The Reunion Planner

The Step-by-Step Guide
Designed to Make Your Reunion
a Social and Financial Success!

Second Edition

Linda Johnson Hoffman
Neal Barnett

Goodman Lauren Publishing   Los Angeles, California

Requests for such permissions should be referred to Publisher:
Goodman Lauren Publishing
www.reunionplanner.com
info@reunionplanner.com

Front and back covers designed by Carol Gravelle
Graphics by Mark Luscombe and Mike Remenih
Illustrations by Elizabeth Aldridge Holmes
Editing by Lisa-Catherine Cohen

Library of Congress Catalog Card Number: 98-74996

Publisher's Cataloging in Publication Data
(Provided by Quality Books, Inc.)
Hoffman, Linda Johnson
    The Reunion Planner: the step-by-step guide designed to make your reunion a social and financial success! / Linda Johnson Hoffman and Neal Barnett. – 2nd ed.
    p. cm.
    Includes bibliographical references and index.
    ISBN: 0-9630516-8-7

    1. Class reunions–Planning. 2. Family reunions–Planning. 3. Reunions–Handbooks, manuals, etc. I. Barnett, Neal. II. Title.

LB3618.H64 1999   371.8'9
                                         QBI98-680

To my husband, Stan and my daughter Lauren, the anchors in my life who provide continual love and inspiration.

Thank you also to my daughter for the following words of wisdom, "If you don't make your reunion interesting, people will never want to come again."

Acknowledgments

This book represents the contributions of many people, including family, friends and fellow reunion enthusiasts. To Michael Remenih, friend and fellow alum, thank you for the many hours and creative donations to our reunions. Your essential help on the computer graphics in this book were extraordinary. To Lisa-Catherine Cohen, thank you for your superb editing. Your invaluable work turned lesser words and sentences into inspiring diction.

To my fellow hardworking reunion committee members Kathy Aberbach, Isabella Barbati, Cindy Crawford, Mark Friedman, Simon Grock, Susan Hershorn, Les Lazar, Lisa Raufman, Robi Robinson and John Vossler who spent many hours working on our high school reunions, thank you for all your enthusiasm and assistance. Without your efforts on our recent 30-year reunion for North Hollywood High School Class of 1967, it would not have been the spectacular event that it was.

The illustrations in this book represent the work and charming nature of Elizabeth Aldridge Holmes. Her pictures brought levity and personality to this guide. To Carol Gravelle who designed the front and back covers, thank you for your patience and diligent efforts and to Mark Luscombe, your graphic assistance on the last page was excellent.

I would like to express my appreciation to the many reunion planners who took the time and effort to respond to the survey from our first effort. Many of your suggestions, experiences and remarks are included herein and credit is given when mentioned.

Neal Barnett, my partner and computer programmer extraordinaire, your efforts and proficiency are what makes this project come together. To your parents, Ron and Connie Barnett, thanks for your reunion planning expertise. Thank you to Patricia Papanek and to your cousin, Barbara Shapley, for your inspiring and imaginative contributions on family reunions. To Don Silver, thank you for your support and many suggestions. They are always so helpful. Thank you to friends and contributors Edna Brock, Samantha Greenberg, Vivian Kahn, Debbie Lawrence, Susan Silver and Frank Wein.

Finally, I would like to thank my wonderful family. To my mother for your constant love and insight. My husband Stan, your enthusiasm, ideas, encouragement and patience are extremely supportive and kept me focused. To my daughter Lauren, your bubbling personality and energy keep me upbeat and on track. You are the essence of my life. I love and thank my family very much.

Contents

1 Year Before the Reunion

9 Months Before the Reunion

Read Me First

I t's time for a reunion! Whether it's a class, family, church, university or military group being reunited, as reunion organizers, we want to make this an absolutely wonderful event. We want attendees to leave convinced that it was the perfect reunion. While we're at it, let's imagine an event that exceeds all expectations.

Sound like ambitious goals? With a little organization and forethought, along with a few enthusiastic volunteers, these aspirations are attainable and well worth all our time and effort.

Of course, those of us who plan reunions realize it takes energy, and lots of it. It represents a labor of love. To be successful, a reunion must: 1) be a memorable experience, 2) raise enough resources to cover all expenses and 3) retain a surplus for the next reunion. Our primary goals are to bring people together again to reminisce, reestablish friendships and appreciate the reunion that rekindled these relationships. This book will help you achieve these objectives.

As the title suggests, this book is designed to help make your reunion a social and financial success. While people who go to their reunions have different expectations, they all want to have a great time. To that end, you must provide more than the basic package, and you don't want to lose money! Any recipe for success calls for planning, organization, cash flow and enthusiasm. If you have the last ingredient, we can help with the rest. The result: a fun-filled, personalized reunion that is organized, well-attended and financially successful.

THE PATH TO SUCCESSFUL PLANNING

Congratulations! In using this book, you have set the plan in motion. Planning a reunion is a unique and gratifying experience, and yes, time consuming in our busy lifestyles. However, planning is the essence of success and this reunion guide provides the tools you need to give you the confidence it takes to plan a sensational reunion. We also show you how to simplify and streamline your efforts by using a computer program to organize all the data.

As the organizer for my 10-year class reunion, before the arrival of personal computers, we did everything by hand. That really took a long time. When it was time for our 20-year reunion, I had lost much of my paperwork and had to recreate almost everything from scratch.

By my next reunion, computers were widely in use. Putting all our alumni data into one, comprehensive database seemed resourceful. Fortunately, at that time, I was working with a systems analyst named Neal Barnett. I asked him if he could write a program that would include all the information I needed. He did, and the result was a program that worked so well, we decided to design one to go along with a book for reunion planners.

Using a Computer

We highly recommend using a computer program. If you don't have one, we suggest you find someone who does to help you. You can store all the details of your group's reunion including names, addresses, phone numbers, location, response status and purchases. Just having a program can be an incentive for planning your reunion. It is much more efficient and convenient than not having one. Throughout this guide, we use computer disk icons to suggest where you might apply our companion computer program or other comparable software.

If You Don't Have a Computer
While a computer definitely makes the job easier, we have designed this book to help reunion committees even when one is not available. Just follow this book from start to finish. A worksheet and sample budget in Chapter 4 will guide you toward a positive ending balance. Create invitations using ideas from the many samples. Computers have become a necessity of life, but don't fret. The old-fashioned way (handwrite, type and draw) may take a little longer, but it still works.

REUNIONS "R" U.S.
Reunions are an important part of our culture. As people get older, they become more nostalgic and have a greater interest in revisiting the past. According to Roper Starch Worldwide of New York City, approximately 7 percent of adult Americans attended a high school, army, college or other reunion in 1995. Reunion Research shows that more than 350,000 class and family reunions are held annually. Military reunions may be less in number, but the incentives and interest in having them might be even stronger.

Soldiers share a special bond but according to Bill Masciangelo, author of the *Military Reunion Handbook,* military reunions are decreasing since 85 percent of military reunions are held by World War II veterans whose members are getting scarce. The potential for military reunions continues to thrive, however, as is evidenced by the numbers. Korean vets number 4.6 million and Vietnam vets make up 8.3 million and are approaching their 25- and 30-year anniversaries. "I was in the Navy during the Korean War and the ship I was on in the early 50s still has reunions every year," according to Enrique T. Tabyanan, reunion organizer for the 70th Air Refueling Association.

Edith Wagner, editor of *Reunions Magazine,* reaffirms this idea based on her research that naval reunions occur more often than any other military service since shipmates formed strong bonds serving on ships in close quarters.

WHAT'S NEW IN THIS EDITION?

First, while the initial edition of *The Reunion Planner* focused on high school reunions, this effort is expanded to include family and military reunions.

Secondly, in spearheading my 30th (and fourth) high school reunion, I discovered many new and exciting ideas. Furthermore, with feedback from the survey in the first edition, the incentive for updating this guide grew even more.

Thirdly, with the immense advances in technology, including tips for finding people on the Internet seemed timely. Finally, a Resource Section was added to provide easy access to reunion vendors and related services.

GETTING THE MOST VALUE FROM THIS BOOK

The Contents outline each chapter's main topics and along with the Index are useful reference tools. Organized by chronological tasks, each chapter takes you step-by-step through the reunion and beyond. *Do not despair if you don't have the recommended time to plan your reunion.* While there is a wealth of ideas throughout the book, just do what you can in the time available. Conversely, if you try to do to much, things may get done carelessly.

Tips and Tricks

To get the most benefit from this guide, focus on those sections that apply to your reunion and follow these suggestions:

- Scan through the entire book first.
- Keep a highlighter and Post-It-Notes ™ handy. Highlight those pages and ideas you may want to refer to later.
- Jot down ideas, questions or thoughts on a notepad and bring them up at future reunion committee meetings. Transfer successful ideas to a task list.
- Reference the book throughout the planning process being sure to concentrate on the relevant time frames.
- Refer to the helpful *Tips* and stories displayed in italics and small print sent in by readers of our first edition.
- Consider getting extra copies of the book for other committee members. (Call publisher for multiple-book discounts.)

Review the chapter outlines below and highlight those areas that most reflect your reunion plan. Chapter 1, _Initial Decisions_, offers incentives to organize your reunion. If you conclude you just don't have the resources to do it on your own, you should consider hiring professional planners. This chapter will show you how to work with professionals and still maintain a personalized reunion. Chapter 2, _Get Organized_, reviews what you can accomplish at committee meetings and proposes when and where to have the event. The _Checklist_ that follows is a handy reminder of all conceivable tasks. Copy these pages, and record items as they're completed. The third chapter addresses the biggest boon in reunion planning since the advent of personal computers . . . finding people on the Internet. Several Websites that offer the most comprehensive value as of this writing are cited. Considering how quickly the information superhighway changes, the only way to keep pace with the latest offerings is to continue checking the Internet, including our Website and others for updates.

Create a money plan using the worksheets in Chapter 4. Setting up a budget and maintaining accurate accounting records is an essential part of the planning process. Doing this early will help prevent financial blunders. In this chapter, you'll learn about planning early fundraisers and how to come up with a suitable ticket price to make certain all expenses are covered with a safety margin. This section includes tips on how to estimate a turnout, and, if you're running short on cash, how to deal with last minute appeals. Chapter 5, _The Foundation_, offers guidance on a first mailing. It also has ideas for ice breakers, activities and games with hints on hiring entertainers, videographers and photographers. Media ads, bank accounts and accounting guidelines complete the basics. _Creating an Ambiance_ is the subject of Chapter 6. Ideas for themes, souvenirs, memory albums and name tags are proposed.

Chapter 7 reflects on how to _Get People There_. Typically accomplished through mailings and phone drives, you'll find more ways to encourage attendance. One of the more difficult aspects to reunion planning is encountering those reluctant to attend. As organizers, we put so much effort into planning the event that it's discouraging to encounter disinterest. This chapter will help planners soothe some perceived fears and anxieties.

Reunion Decor is reviewed in Chapter 8. Topics include decorations, displays and memorabilia along with advice on what items to sell at reunions. Chapter 9 focuses on family and military reunion specifics. It offers reunion locations, games and activities, souvenirs, awards and fundraising. Genealogy research and family histories as they can be developed at reunions are covered in Chapter 10. Chapter 11 has program and award suggestions. Chapter 12 examines how to organize an effective registration process. Chapters 13 and 14 sketch out a weekend reunion and discuss closing costs and responsibilities. Lastly, Chapter 15 relates how to stay up to date with reunion planning.

Our first edition included a survey asking readers to send in their reunion stories and experiences. Planners from all over the country who used our guide responded to our survey. We heard what worked and what didn't, the pitfalls and the victories. We received samples of newsletters and announcements. Sprinkled throughout are quotes and stories from some of these letters.

WE WANT MORE OF YOUR FEEDBACK!

Please continue to send us your reunion experiences. We would especially like to know how you overcame difficulties and solved problems. Just photocopy the Survey toward the end of this book, fill it out and send or fax it to us so we can include your input in our next edition. Our address and phone numbers are on the last page of this book. Quicker yet, respond to our Survey directly on our Website: ***www.reunionplanner.com.*** Help us continue the journey in helping others create wonderful reunions.

Our Website also offers other reunion products and services. We even point you to related Websites. If you have questions or comments regarding anything in this book or the companion computer software, simply contact us through our Website.

No matter what the economic climate, rain or shine, reunions will go on. They are distinct events that allow us to revisit special moments in our lives and, in fact, become milestones themselves. We need the special handful of people like you who take the initiative to bring the rest of us together. Completing this process becomes rewarding beyond measure for so many others, and, it becomes a fabulous experience for you.

1
Initial Decisions
Who, What, Where, When and Why

R eunions. Creating them or simply attending them trigger many emotions in us. They can invoke happy memories, nostalgic reflections and a desire to rekindle old friendships with whom we shared important life experiences. They can also provoke squeamishness from those who did not have the most wonderful of pasts.

As we have said, it is a precious few who are willing to take on the challenge of planning such events. If you are reading this book, you are likely one of the dedicated. Despite a natural apprehension, you may still be experiencing some trepidations: "How can I find the time?" "I don't know anyone who could help right now." "This is just too huge an undertaking." or, "I don't know where to begin." Since you are in possession of this book, you've already made the first commitment and are well on the way toward creating a great reunion!

During high school, I was secretary of my senior class. I never thought about reunions back then, nor did I think it was my responsibility to organize them. But nine years after our graduation, recognizing that someone had to start the process if we were to have a reunion, I took the initiative.

In my professional career, I had participated in the planning of many large entertainment events – political dinners, fundraisers and charity functions – so I must admit that my first foray into the idea of planning my reunion was instinctive and even fun. Our first reunion, 10 years after graduation, turned out fabulously. Now I had the information and know-how to go on to organize our 20-, 25- and 30-year reunions. The first edition of this book was written following my 20-year reunion. Creating it served as a guide for subsequent reunions.

Why *You* Should Take the Initiative

It costs people a lot of energy AND money to just get to a reunion. So expectations naturally run high. That's a big responsibility to take on and a lot to live up to. Nevertheless, by the time you finish this chapter, if you are not thoroughly convinced you're ready to take the plunge and start making those phone calls, consider hiring professional reunion planners. Once you have one reunion under your belt, the basics will be in place for the next one. If it helps, remember that you can reduce your involvement later on, but somebody needs to initiate the process.

How to Find Time in Your Busy Schedule to Plan this Event

▸ Organize an effective reunion committee, one that works well together.

▸ Plan and prioritize.

▸ Take advantage of this reunion "how to" book for shortcuts, ideas and guidelines.

▸ Try to keep egos out of the way and incorporate the talents and energies of other committee members.

▸ Ask family members to help out, it will be fun for them too.

▸ Use committee meetings and reunion projects as opportunities for learning computer graphics, enhancing your writing talents and working on time management skills.

TOP 10 REASONS TO PLAN YOUR REUNION

1. People look forward to reunions. They will really be grateful for all your efforts on their behalf.

2. The event will be more personal.

3. Gain self-esteem and satisfaction upon completion of this important event.

4. Reestablish friendships. You have the opportunity to reconnect at length with friends and family members from by-gone days, more so than if you only attend a reunion.

5. Enjoy the comradarie of working with a committee toward a common goal. You get to reminisce in the process.

6. Enjoy mini-reunions during the phone drive. You'll find yourself immersed in conversations with former classmates or family members whom you haven't spoken to in a long time.

7. Receive tremendous gratification knowing you've brought people together who might otherwise never have seen each other again.

8. Seize the opportunity to put together a genealogy chart, family history or other permanent record you always wished you had.

9. Provide networking opportunities for family and friends.

10. Savor the memories for many years to come.

Bonus. You will find that invitees are more likely to respond positively to a phone call or letter from a classmate, family member or military buddy who is contacting them.

Hiring Professional Planners May Be Worth Considering

Before hiring anyone, make a list of the pros and cons.

Pros of Pros	Cons of Pros
Up-front Costs They take care of the necessary deposits and initial expenses.	With less effort than you might expect, you can raise money to cover those expenses in a variety of interesting ways: 1. Collect advance ticket money from members of your committee. 2. Plan a small fund raiser before your reunion. 3. Ask if you can pay deposits in installments as you collect money. Most establishments will happily work with you.
Finding People They do this for you.	Now more than ever, finding people is easy. And fun. By far, the bulk of your time will be spent finding people. The Internet has completely changed the landscape of reunion planning. With instant access to current home, business phone numbers and E-mail addresses of people all over the globe, the Internet has made the task of finding lost alumni, family and friends faster, cheaper and totally efficient. For those who have E-mail, communication has become streamlined and timesaving. Virtually at your fingertips, the computer has made the available search range international in scope. Again, old friends and relatives will be more responsive to real alumni and family members than to strangers. Also, the experience of finding people from your past turns out to be very valuable.

Pros of Pros	Cons of Pros
Mailings They send out all mailings.	Make a party out of it! All you need is a big space in someone's home or office. With 5-10 people, the mailings can be stuffed, stamped and addressed in no time.
Registration You may not abhor sitting at the check-in table the first time, but when the next reunion rolls around, you won't want to be stuck there.	Delegate! Organize short shifts. People will be glad to take turns. No one expects you to carry the load. Perhaps the spouses of the committee members will help. It'll give them something to do for the first hour.

If you find you are just not able to devote the time to such a project right now and you definitely want a reunion to happen, hire a professional reunion planner. Even if you work with professional planners, this book will help you have a more successful reunion. Stay as active in the planning process as your time allows. Form your own committee. Authorize the contents of all mailings. It is also a good idea to oversee mailings and other reunion items.

The National Association of Reunion Managers (NARM) is a non-profit organization of professional reunion companies. Their members must follow strict industry standards with regard to contracts and communications with alumni committees and high schools. You can register your reunion on their Website and find professional reunion planners among their members in your area. Their toll-free number is 1(800) 654-2776 and their Website address is: *http://www.reunions.com.*

Certain companies specialize in finding people. Always make absolutely sure the organization or single professional you hire has good references. We have heard of fabulously-planned reunions as well as those in which professional planners disappeared right before the reunion, taking thousands of dollars in reunion ticket revenue with them! Therefore, we offer you the following guidelines in engaging anyone:

Get References

Check the Yellow Pages, the Internet or call a high school for names of companies that have organized successful reunions for other classes. Before you hire anyone, ask them for references from other reunion committees who have used them.

Check Them Out

1. Meet with them. Ask to see photos of other reunions they have organized.

2. Look at their portfolio. Look at sample mailings, name tags and photo albums. Ask to attend a reunion they are currently planning. This will really help you visualize your event.

3. Check out their insurance liability carrier and see that their policies are current.

Make Sure the Contract with Them Includes *Your* Conditions

When you are ready to sign a contract, be sure it reflects your interests and includes the following conditions:

▸ Secure a bond (like an escrow account) payable to the class committee or create a joint account should the company fail to perform. You could lose a lot of money, and all the time and effort, if the company dissolves before your event. (Heaven forbid!)

▸ The committee is to be given copies of any alumni lists the professional planner has developed, including names, addresses and phone numbers. (Updates might not be easy to obtain from them, since herein lies the basis for securing your future business.)

▸ You shall get all responses (read them yourself) received from the Missing Persons list as well as the returned, filled out questionnaires. This way you can follow up on leads the professionals might not pursue.

▸ You must be allowed to contribute and have final approval on the design and content of mailings and other related items. The professionals must include your names to legitimatize their efforts, so your input on all reunion materials is necessary.

▸ If you don't like any of them, you don't have to settle for the choices they offer for places to hold your reunion. Be aware of the fact that reunion companies have prior deals with particular venues, caterers, entertainment and photographers.

▸ Your committee is to be given the complementary overnight rooms offered by most hotels to groups holding large events there.

▸ Name tags must include yearbook pictures! (If their "package" does not include this essential memento, insist on it or have them refund a portion of each ticket price. Then make your own. Like we said, in our experience, pictures are essential.)

▸ After the reunion, the photographer must send the photo proofs directly to your committee. (This guarantees your possession of the reunion pictures should the organizers not follow through with this final task.)

▸ Stay closely involved in all aspects of decision-making, including the selection of table centerpieces, door prizes and souvenirs. Your ideas will result in a more personalized event.

There are many good professional planners in the marketplace. But you have to stay alert. While they may sell themselves as the answer to all your worries, consider that for them to be profitable, they have to juggle several reunions at once. Their highest priority just might not be you. Shop around and hire the one whom you feel truly understands your vision.

Whether you decide to plan your own reunion or hire professional planners, get started right away! The sooner, the better. Once the first meeting happens and everyone is excited and bursting with anticipation, you will know you've made the right decision.

WHY REUNIONS ARE SO IMPORTANT

Planning my reunions has always been a very satisfying experience. As an organizer, it is not just a fleeting event. It becomes an ongoing opportunity to really connect with people in my past. Then the past becomes the present.

During my most recent reunion, I discovered something more. Planning these events were not only enjoyable experiences, they were essential components of my life. Much of the self respect I feel today comes from reliving and understanding my past through each reunion planning undertaking.

I love the long conversations that allow me to catch up with those whom I shared my formative years. I enjoy hearing new stories and anecdotes. And, for the first time since high school, I got to reminisce with my first date. Now that was invigorating! In chatting with an alum I had known since Junior High School, I heard a wonderful story about my now deceased father. I was also impressed with the hardships many of my classmates endured, and yes, heartened by how we all survived.

The reunion gave me the opportunity to reunite with friends with whom I had lost touch. Best of all, I got to know and care about many people I hadn't had the occasion to know in school.

Finally, a former teacher, Mr. Dick Bell, who attended our 25th reunion put into perspective much of what reunions have come to represent.

> *Many of you have attended not only high school together, but junior high and sometimes even grammar school. In your transition from childhood to adolescence, you shared many experiences both painful and triumphant and in many ways left an indelible imprint on each other.*

A reunion is a celebration of life; not just your life, but the lives of all those around you. It offers you an opportunity to revisit a period of your past that had so much influence in guiding you to become who you are today. It is an affirmation of your successful transition from youth to maturity, and the good news is, you have survived. Many of these people share that triumph with you tonight. These are such infrequent yet very important opportunities in your life. Thank you for letting me share this moment with you tonight. I encourage you to attend all your school reunions.

Doesn't this apply to any group that shared significant life experiences? Cousins from opposite coasts planned their Italian family reunion in August 1995. Barbara Shapley from Florida along with her cousin, Patricia Papanek of California, organized a reunion in New York. After the event, in a letter to her family, Barbara made the following observations:

Our family reunion was "a happenin." Laughing, playing kazoos, card games, boccie ball, watching old videos and greeting each new carload of cousins, we reflected on our lives and the lives of all of those gone before us. We cried and hugged each other. We learned so many stories, shared so many perceptions, but best of all, we know who we are, and why we are, and how we are. We have so much more to tell.

IN SUMMARY, THREE KEY POINTS

1. Get Adequate Assistance.

The number of volunteers who really pitch in determine the success of your event. The more people searching and hence, finding, former classmates, family and friends, the higher your turnout. A continual flow of ideas and enthusiasm, plus clear lines of communication make the process move along smoothly. In an atmosphere of harmony and focus, the job becomes more like a social gathering than work.

2. Plan and Prioritize.

Set your priorities and goals. That structure is essential to any successful endeavor. You need to be able to make decisions, organize well, budget properly and follow through on tasks.

The successful reunion will happen based upon the time you and other volunteers commit to it. Organizing your time and resources for this project is Step one. Author Susan Silver, *Organized to be the Best!* explains that, "Time management is the foundation of good organization." You need to "take the time to plan and prioritize" to be successful in achieving your goals. Research indicates that every hour of planning saves three or more hours.

The Elements of Effective Reunion Organization

3. Enter Your Data in a Computer Program.

Computerizing your alumni and guest information is a time and labor saving device. The program that was designed along with this book will help you gain that end. All areas of reunion planning benefit from this tool. Recommended usage of the program is identified by computer icons throughout this book.

1 Year
Before the Reunion

2

Get Organized

The ABCs of Organization:
Strategize, Structure and Streamline

Three basic steps in achieving organizational excellence and realizing your goals can be summed up in three words: *Strategize, Structure and Streamline.* This kind of advance planning will pay for itself when you're dancing at your fabulous reunion. Insufficient planning can't help but result in a so-so event.

A. STRATEGIZE: *Come up With Resourceful Ways of Accomplishing Your Goals*

Making key contacts is the beginning of this process. That includes forming an effective committee with people you know will get the job done.

ESTABLISH THE REUNION COMMITTEE

Form a committee to begin planning the event. Start this at least one year in advance. While there are usually one or two persons from any group who will initiate a reunion drive, we recommend a committee be formed for assistance in all other aspects of planning.

In most groups, one person usually emerges who has the willingness and capability to lead. This person will typically chair the reunion committee and oversee all the tasks. To prevent burn-out and maintain sanity, you don't want to laden one person with all the responsibility. Try to delegate tasks and divide the labor.

Be aware that some people come to committee meetings whose only interest is in socializing and reminiscing. You must be assertive to help everyone stay on track. Assign very specific tasks and due dates. This is good practice and helpful for everyone involved. There are several tasks that committee members can handle:

1. Searching for people
2. Maintaining the main address list or database
3. Preparing mailers and announcements
4. Editing the alumni/family histories for the memory album
5. Putting a memory album/photo book together
6. Making menu/meal arrangements
7. Selecting entertainment
8. Planning activities and games
9. Organizing a pre-event fund raiser
10. Raising funds for a social action project
11. Sending acknowledgment postcards and/or reminder notices
12. Managing the media announcements
13. Preparing pictures, slides or a video as a reunion display
14. Arranging for door prizes
15. Getting a banner
16. Ordering T-shirts and other fundraising items
17. Making the photo name tags
18. Preparing registration packets
19. Creating a business directory or business card handout
20. Designing a survey
21. Setting up a memorabilia table
22. Assembling table centerpieces
23. Designing decorations and displays

24. Producing an event program
25. Selecting and ordering souvenirs
26. Organizing a charitable donation
27. Planning a picnic or other informal events

The group energy of a committee is what maintains that infectious enthusiasm. In building a committee, choose those people who have the time, talent and a genuine interest in making your reunion work.

▸ Alumni/family/co-horts you keep in touch with whom you know will be enthusiastic

▸ Some may have already contacted the school or military registry office

▸ Retired family members

▸ Former class officers, prior reunion committee members

▸ Alumni association membership

▸ Those who expressed an interest during the phone drive

At one meeting during the phone drive, we located Cindy. When she heard we were planning a reunion, she immediately wanted to help. She drove right over and became our most enthusiastic volunteer, calling alumni and encouraging them to attend. She also enlisted another alum to help on the committee.

In establishing meeting times, consider that a lot can be accomplished in just two or three meetings geared to collecting seed money, conducting the people search and handling mailings. Someone's office will be very handy since everyone can go to a phone to make calls and be in one place to compare results. If you have more volunteers than phones, delegate the other tasks to those not making calls.

Volunteers can also call and search the Web at home. If phone lists are given to people to take home, make sure you select people you trust will follow through and fax or mail their results to the person responsible for updating the primary list.

To maximize your results and reduce time and effort spent alone, ask for enough assistance. One or two people will likely emerge as the leaders and take responsibility for important tasks. If you surface as the leader of your group, have a task checklist (pages 20-21) or use the computer program printout described here to identify and assign specific tasks. Then follow-up to see that tasks are getting done, especially the most time-consuming one: finding people.

> ■ **Under To-Do Lists, print lists for each person with their assignment, the date given and the due date.**
> ■ **Mark dates when completed.**

The main focus at the first meeting should be on accomplishing two goals, collecting seed money and organizing the search for missing persons.

Collecting Seed Money

Since there will be postage, phone and stationery costs as well as deposits on the hotel and entertainment, the committee is going to need some initial financing.

▸ The easiest and quickest method is to ask committee members to pay for their tickets up-front or to lend money to the reunion bank account.

▸ Arrange an early fundraiser that won't require much work. This will also stimulate interest on the upcoming reunion. Charge a small fee above the meal or event cost. Hold it at an inexpensive restaurant, committee members' home or other entertainment venue. One class reunion committee from Van Nuys, California planned a small event six months before their reunion:

> We held a small spaghetti dinner fundraiser at a local Italian restaurant and charged $25.00 a person. Announcements for this event, which was limited to 100 persons, were included with the

first reunion mailing. It was a huge success and, in fact, was sold out.

▸ Offer incentives such as deadlines for early ticket purchases, discounts or payment installments. This will require meticulous bookkeeping, but will effectively cover the initial costs.

▸ Charge a fee for advertising business cards in the next reunion mailing. This is a win-win situation. It is an easy money raiser and is an inexpensive advertising vehicle to a predisposed receptive audience.

▸ Attract corporate/community sponsorship. Solicit local businesses that might have a connection or affinity toward your group. Offer them advertising incentives.

▸ Promote an early auction in mailers. Offer at least 10 items such as the free hotel room at the reunion event. Solicit hotels, stores, services, professional sports venues and restaurants to contribute. The highest bidders from the first 25 respondents win. It's good advertising for participating companies.

▸ Send out annual newsletters to your group and charge a subscription fee. Newsletters are easy to produce in word processing templates. (A newsletter front page is in Chapter 5.)

▸ Order T-shirts and other mementos with your family or class name and charge an amount over the cost of the shirt. Depending on the amount you order, there are many T-shirt vendors that offer lower rates for large quantities. These make great souvenirs. Have your school logo, family crest, even old photos with class, family or military photos printed on them. Such mementos can be purchased at your school's student store, reunion sites on the Internet or through catalogues.

▸ Organize a pot luck meal, pancake breakfast, chili cook-off or dessert party in a committee member's backyard, at a park or in a community center. Charge a per person fee, offer discounts to children and encourage family attendance.

▸ Save money on initial printing costs by requesting in-kind donations in lieu of ticket payments. For example, a committee member may have a print shop or know of someone that can provide a discount on printing costs on stationery, name tags, mailings or personalized tickets. You could also barter with free ads in your reunion literature.

Include an agenda in the committee meeting notices (see sample below) that can be mailed or faxed to members prior to each meeting. This will let people know what to expect so that they can bring the necessary materials and set their calendars accordingly.

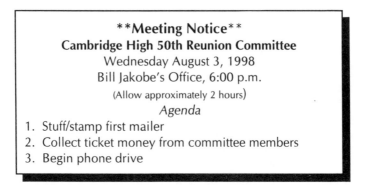

Meeting Notice
Cambridge High 50th Reunion Committee
Wednesday August 3, 1998
Bill Jakobe's Office, 6:00 p.m.
(Allow approximately 2 hours)
Agenda
1. Stuff/stamp first mailer
2. Collect ticket money from committee members
3. Begin phone drive

Organizing the Search for Missing Persons

If you have a large list of names, begin by dividing the phone lists among all committee members into groups, such as A-E and F-L, etc. *Request that updated addresses retrieved from everyone's search is legible!* Remind callers to ask for the whereabouts of other "missing persons" during telephone conversations. Offer to reimburse volunteers for home-originated long-distance charges.

■ **If volunteers are making calls from home, print out phone lists by area code.**
■ **If calls are being made at one location, print out the entire phone list alphabetically.**

YOUR OLD STOMPING GROUNDS

For class reunions, go to your school. The school serves as the central headquarters which is an important link for alumni information. By paying a personal visit you can see the lay of the land, take pictures, get alumni lists and you never know what other useful materials you can gather. You could even encounter a former teacher or two which won't happen if you only call. Here are some things to look for:

Names and Addresses

Check to see whether any of the following lists exist:

▸ A graduation list

▸ A diploma list

▸ Enrollment cards

▸ Any information with dates of birth, military unit or rank

▸ Any data with the first names of both parents. Parents especially are less likely to have moved.

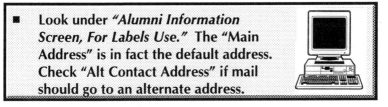

■ **Look under** *"Alumni Information Screen, For Labels Use."* **The "Main Address" is in fact the default address. Check "Alt Contact Address" if mail should go to an alternate address.**

Doris Taylor organized her 50th Dunbar Senior High School reunion in Baltimore, Maryland. As a member of the Membership Committee of the Alumni Association, she had access to the membership list. With her continued contact with her school, she could enjoy the 1998 graduating class acknowledging her 1948 class at their ceremonial graduation.

School Reunion Coordinator

Usually high schools and colleges have assigned a faculty member to handle reunion inquiries. Meet with this person. He or she will aid in making sure alumni are properly informed about your reunion. You will also meet the administration staff and ensure that everyone is familiar with your group's reunion.

Tour of the Grounds
If you live far away from your school, hometown, church or former military base, request pictures of the area as it looked at the time and take photos of how it looks now. These enlarged photos can make for great displays at your reunion or include them in mailings and newsletters.

Memorabilia
Check the main office, Chambers of Commerce, the local Historical Society, military base or on-site stores for articles to be raffled off, displayed or used as door prizes or souvenirs. With an added caption or logo, you can create T-shirts, sweatshirts, hats, glassware or pencils. Search for old newspaper articles, newsletters, songsheets, yearbooks, stuffed animals, sports bottles or other items.
Here is Jackie Diamond's story from a visit to her high school in Sun Valley, California:

> When I began planning my 25th high school reunion, I visited the school and got even more information than I had from previous visits. (I already had the graduation list from our 10th reunion). I met the reunion coordinator who was very helpful. She gave me copies of our school song and other memorabilia. I also had a wonderful encounter with a former teacher and invited her to attend our reunion.
> The student store had stuffed animal replicas of our school mascot which I bought for table centerpieces . I also got T-shirts, pencils and notebooks for mementos and door prizes. A greater find was their last copy of our senior yearbook. Knowing it would be in high demand by alumni who had since lost theirs, I bought it and auctioned it off at our reunion.

Continue the Contact Throughout the Year
This "home base" is an important link for people who have been out of touch. To facilitate this conduit and prevent any potential misinformation, send your school, military base, church or association notices about your reunion periodically, i.e.,

- Flyers with your reunion information

- If there is no school reunion coordinator, call periodically to verify that information being distributed about your reunion is correct! Administrative staff persons change and your reunion details could get lost in the process.

- Copies of local media ads

- Ask your organization to post a notice on their outdoor marquis or billboard.

THE SCHOOL CAN HELP TOO!

There are a few things a school can do to help this process along and create good will at the same time. It would be clever, forward thinking for the high school reunion coordinator or alumni association to prepare a reunion packet for each graduating class. The packet (now computer disk) should contain the names, parent's names, addresses and phone numbers of graduating seniors with one copy kept at the school and another given to a class officer (who usually are the ones initiating reunions). What a wonderful gift to the class! Not only would this establish an alumni list for future reunion committees, it also creates fundraising potential for the school. If you are organizing a class reunion, pass this suggestion on to your high school and tell them to spread the word among other schools.

WHAT HAPPENS IF THE SCHOOL NO LONGER EXISTS?

You are at a distinct disadvantage if your alma mater no longer exists or if address records have been lost or destroyed. If no one can locate a class list, there are other methods to try. First, check to see if your former school has an alumni association. Even when schools close down, alumni associations have been known to continue for many years and maintain records. You might only have a few names from your class, but at least some addresses are likely to be current. If you have access to the Internet, the alumni association could have a Website.

▸   Many a reunion has been planned based solely on the names and pictures in the yearbook. This is actually a great starting point for the first phone drive meeting. (See pages 20-21 for other committee member assignments to be delegated while you are searching through phone books and dialing phone Information.)

Vivian Kahn of Hayward, California offers the following suggestion:

Tip: *People are always asking whether you remember "so-and-so" or know the whereabouts of someone, so bring yearbooks to all committee meetings. Having the yearbook handy will bring back many a forgotten face with the asked-about name.*

▸   Contact alumni associations for nearby colleges, previous class reunion committees or yearbook distributors.

▸   Remember to check out your commencement program.

▸   If an alumni association does not exist, check into starting one and charge nominal membership dues to pay for printing and postage. Keep everyone updated and maintain contact. Doris Fantini, a reunion planner from Somerville, Maine did exactly that.

Doris is an alumnus from a small parochial school. She contacted us after her 35th Notre Dame High School Reunion. In 1972, her school closed after 65 years and there was no location to go to and get former records. In 1986, after serving on a committee for a school-wide reunion and fundraiser, she decided an alumni association was needed. So, 5 years later in 1991 with a handful of volunteers and a Board of 9 to 11 members, she established an alumni association. While sometimes difficult, it's much more often rewarding and she has maintained it ever since.

Our association publishes the Stella Maris (the name of the school yearbook) Newsletter twice a year which highlights recent achievements of our alumni and teachers, announcements of social events being planned and reunion encouragement. We charge $20 yearly membership dues to cover printing, postage *and miscellaneous costs. We also plan free social gatherings which are great opportunities to plan class reunions and sponsored fundraising events for the Sisters.*

She also keeps a "class rep" program going with at least one class member per year to act as a contact for follow-up reunions and as a link to/for missing alumni. The association recognizes special alumni occasions, finds sponsors for gifts for celebrations and sends thank yous for participating. They conduct interviews and surveys for publication in their newsletter. Both goals—continuing alumni contact and providing financial aide to the Sisters of the Holy Union—filled needs on several fronts.

Only truly inspired alumni take the time to get involved to this extent, but the endeavor can be an inspiring and satisfying experience. Perks, like the satisfaction and enjoyment derived by:

▸ maintaining regular contact with everyone (which in turn keeps the mailing list current),

▸ knowing there is a central "home base" for all alumni and reunion-related communications,

▸ providing an ongoing source of funds for reunions and related fundraising activities,

▸ promoting perpetual interest, affinity and networking opportunities for alumni and family.

B. STRUCTURE: *Set up the Framework*

A structure is determined by deciding when and where to have your reunion. To gather input from your invitees on preferences for dates and locations, send out a questionnaire. Venues are booked at least a year in advance, so 18 months to 2 years is an appropriate lead time to send out a questionnaire.

Date and Theme

The date for your reunion will be determined by your chosen location's availability and estimated attendance. Class reunions are typically planned during the summer months: June through

September. Nevertheless, don't feel limited; if winter or spring turns out to be more convenient for the majority of attendees, choose the most desirable date.

Summer dates enable families to plan vacations around school breaks. Year-end holidays or 3-day weekends are ideal times for family reunions. Some resorts, airlines and hotels have off-season, reduced rates.

While a theme party may not be typical, it offers a variation on the usual routine. You could plan your reunion around a holiday, nostalgia, special family birthday, anniversary or other commemorative event. Some ideas:

▸ A "dress-as-you-were then" party

▸ Holiday-of-the-month theme: Fourth of July, Halloween, Valentine's Day, Mother's or Father's Day

▸ A theme that has significance for your class era or family history: 1950s Sock Hop, Fred and Martha's 50th wedding anniversary, Uncle Jerry's 80th birthday or Jason's christening.

▸ Be different! Have fun! Choose an unusual theme that will allow guests to dress up accordingly: country western, all black and white, disco, rock 'n' roll, a tropical island, carnival, ragtime, Caribbean, masquerade or Roaring 20s. Use this as a focal point for planning food and decorations. Hotels might even have accessories and backdrops to rent. Kathryn Wentland of Wisconsin planned her 20-year high school reunion on a luau theme and designed the menu, decorations and souvenirs Hawaiian style. Leis were handed out to each attendee.

▸ Center your reunion around a related special event: museum opening, school dedication ceremony, ship commissioning or religious occasion.

If you are from a small town or had a relatively small graduating class or military unit, consider organizing an all school/group event where overlapping classes can attend. This accommodates friendships across or between a broader range of ages. Joy Malone Dudgeon of Illinois wrote us that her small English school in an almost all French city, Trois-Rivières, Québec, Canada held a kindergarten-through-high-school reunion. In fact, anyone who had attended the school or had even been their close friends anytime since the school started were invited.

Laurel Hall (a Lutheran-based elementary through high school in North Hollywood, California) organized a 50th Anniversary weekend that invited anyone whoever attended the school. The gala weekend began with a Friday night dinner/dance banquet and silent auction at a nice restaurant. Saturday consisted of a fine arts reunion barbeque and block party where former members of the school band and choir performed. A pot-luck meal was organized and videos from past musicals were shown. Volleyball was played and former teachers hosted the event. Sunday culminated with a alumni choir performance, an open house and luncheon. The total weekend cost was $50 per person and/or an item for the auction.

The Location

If you expect to have a large estimated attendance, for example 200, choose a place accustomed to dealing with groups your size. Hotels with large banquet facilities are the most popular and the most ideal places to hold reunions since everything you need is already there on the premises. The original estimate determines the site selection and affects every other decision.

Depending upon your chosen venue, in making that choice, factor in the costs of either preparing food on-site or hiring an outside caterer. If it doesn't matter, the next decision on the agenda is the caterer. In computing costs, add tables, chairs, linens, dishes, silverware and glassware. (See sample budget in next chapter.)

The primary consideration to bear in mind in making these initial choices is to create a comfortable environment and a conducive atmosphere in which people will feel relaxed enough to reconnect. Everything else is secondary. It doesn't have to be a really expensive dinner/dance! Whatever you choose, base the decision on how much the budget allows. Preparing a preliminary budget is extremely helpful. (Review Chapter 4, *Create a Budget*, before making the final decision on where to hold your reunion.)

When shopping for prospective places in which to hold your reunion, bring a list of questions (see below). Besides price, your selection will be based upon the look and size of the meeting rooms, nearby lodging, restaurants, etc., convenience of location, parking ease, the size of the reception area—just the overall "feel" of the surroundings.

Again, your estimated turnout determines your room size requirement. Copy and bring the following list of all the specifics when visiting potential reunion locations.

Questions for the Catering Manager

1. Look at all the available rooms. Do any of them have the ambiance you want? Are there outdoor facilities, views, smaller meeting rooms? Does it feel spacious enough? Too spacious? Are there windows? How and where can a dance floor be set up?

2. Look at the menu selections and prices. Is there the serving option of food stations or buffets as opposed to the usual sit-down dinner? *What is the complete total price per person including tax and tip?*

3. If the deposit requirement is higher than your current cash flow can accommodate, can the deposit be paid in installments?

4. What are the cancellation procedures? Do they require a signed contract? How much are you liable for in the event that your reunion gets canceled?

5. Is there a separation between the reception area and the dining room? If not, may you use rented lattice or somehow divide these areas? Is there a front registration area? This is a big plus as it allows for a smooth check-in process.

6. Are there any restrictions, rules and/or time limitations for setting up the room/s? Is there a time limit for how late you can play/perform loud music? What is the quitting time for bartenders, servers, cleanup crew? Do they offer and can you pay for extended hours?

7. Can we bring in our own liquor?

8. Is there a cash minimum for bar sales, and how much is charged if the minimum is not met? Will the committee be reimbursed a percentage of the bar sales sold above a base amount?

9. What overage above the guaranteed meal count is allowable for unexpected guests? Are there food choices available for people on restricted diets?

10. Is there a clear and spacious area for the photographer to accommodate the inevitable long lines for the initial individual pictures?

11. (Non-hotel/restaurant sites) Do they use specific vendors?

12. Are there any additional costs? Are things like a dance floor, reception tables, chairs, storage facilities considered "extras" and are you charged as such?

13. Can a podium, bulletin boards, movable blackboards, sign posts and easels be provided?

14. What is the smoking policy?

15. Is there wheelchair accessibility?

16. Can your staff hang a banner for us? Where? Can we put up posters and other decorations on walls?

17. When can outside vendors make their deliveries?

18. Is there a designated spot and sufficient electrical outlets and power to accommodate your sound system?

19. What type of sound system, audio visual equipment, TV, VCRs or microphones are provided? If none, can we bring our own and will there be a staff person to oversee the equipment?

20. Are there enough highchairs and booster seats?

21. If a slide show is planned, can a projector and screen be provided? Is this another extra?

22. Is there an additional fee for the room if people want to stay later?

23. Do you have vendor suggestions for bands, disc jockeys, photographers, florists, etc.?

24. (Hotels only) Is a free guestroom and/or hospitality suite offered with the event? Negotiate for the maximum discount room rate. What is the latest possible reservation cut-off date?

25. Does the hotel have a brochure with directions we may include in our mailings? Pictures or maps can be copied or scanned and placed in reunion mailings.

26. (Non hotel) What are the nearby out-of-town accommodations?

27. When is the final head count and payment due?

28. Hat and coat check in?

29. Do you require liability insurance?

30. Do you have parking lot guards or security guards patrolling the area during the reunion?

31. Is there valet, self or free parking? If so, what is the cost?

32. _____

_____

33. _____

_____

There are other factors besides cost that determine your reunion spot. Is this place close to your school or other nostalgic location? Where is the largest concentration of family members? Is it near a major airport? A minor airport? Is it easy to get to? Difficult? What activities interest your group? Are there facilities for them nearby? Choices of services, restaurants, tourist attractions? Lots of reasons will affect your eventual decision.

Once you find the perfect place, reserve it promptly. If you've chosen May or June for your reunion, remember that these months are popular for weddings, proms and graduation parties, and are scooped up far in advance.

Don't make a hasty decision either. Since you don't want to chance losing the perfect place, don't be forced into making a quick decision. Location managers want your business as much as you want to book a location. Perhaps you can temporarily reserve the room while looking at other sites. Once you find the perfect spot, be sure to notify any other sites you may have put on hold.

Eleanor Schachter of St. Mary's High School said the restaurant they chose did not have a large enough reception area. Inaccurate estimates can have disastrous results. Being forewarned and forearmed is better.

Before you sign on the dotted line, make sure all the verbal conditions such as price, deposit dates and services along with complimentary rooms and other "extras" agreed upon are in writing. If you feel it warranted, you can, as we have said, have a lawyer look it over first. Perhaps someone in your committee knows a lawyer that can donate some time.

We highly recommend a visit to a similar event being held there. This will provide invaluable insight on how your event will appear and perhaps avoid any pitfalls. You might also get some decorating ideas.

Negotiating Points

Some prices might be negotiable, once you're definitely interested. It usually works better to seem as though you're still shopping. Explain that you are a volunteer, non-profit committee, and you might be able to get their non-profit rate. If you have a record of what was spent on your last reunion and the number of rooms that were reserved, you will be better prepared to negotiate.

Ask for reduced rates on parking too. Based on your needs, compare locations' benefits before you negotiate the deal. If you don't ask, you won't get.

REUNION LOCATIONS

Restaurants/Hotels/Country Clubs

These are obvious first choices since they have convenient ballrooms and banquet facilities. These establishments usually have different group rates for the ballroom, overnight rooms and meals. Use your reservation to negotiate for a hospitality suite, extra tables and chairs, bulletin boards and audio visual equipment.

In choosing a menu, be sure to add sales tax and gratuity when determining the total cost per person. A sample menu might look like this:

Dinner cost:	$25.00
Sales tax @ 8%:	2.00
Gratuity @ 17%:	4.60
Total cost per person:	**$31.60**

Another advantage to having your reunion at a hotel is the free overnight room or hospitality suite usually provided to groups holding major events there. Hotels may also offer a free overnight room per a certain block of reserved rooms, usually 20-40. The committee can use the complimentary room to coordinate the flow of the event and to change clothes.

For Guests Staying Overnight at a Hotel

You will get a better reduced overnight room rate for your group if you can convince them your group will bring in at least 20 rooms. Most hotels will block out rooms at a discount rate by a certain date, without a financial commitment on your part. After that date, the going rate kicks back in.

Tip: Welcome guests staying overnight with a courtesy gift. The Red Lion Hotel in Glendale, California presented a welcome note with information on the accommodations and the hospitality suite available to reunion guests. The note accompanied a basket prepared by the committee filled with a small snack, the reunion itinerary and a memento.

As the event nears, ask the hotel for a list of your group's registered guests. Give each guest a copy.

Dinner Theaters, Clubs, Theme Parks

Many theme parks (e.g. Disneyland, Sea World, Disney World, Universal Studios) and dinner theaters have "party packages" which include lists of entertainers, video specialists, etc.

Negotiate a group discount rate at nearby hotels, motels or Bread and Breakfast places for guests who require overnight accommodations. You may be able to arrange free shuttle service to and from the reunion site if enough rooms are reserved. Again, the advantage of these locations is that food and other requisites are included in the per-person meal charge.

Mansions/Estates/Museums/Art Galleries

This idea offers a welcome alternative to the typical, ballroom location and adds just the spark that makes your reunion sizzle. This is usually a more expensive option, however, since food, refreshments, servers, tables and chairs, dance floor and event insurance must be brought in from outside and that adds up. Chambers of Commerce should have a list of mansions, estates or designer showcase homes rentable for a one night affair. Museums and art galleries often make their premises available for events.

The example below uses a 200-person estimate for what additional expenses might be incurred under this option. (Centerpieces, decorations, photo books, etc. are not included since you would still have these costs at a hotel/restaurant.)

Location rental: $2,650.00
Catered meal 6,000.00
   (Including servers, utensils, plates, napkins, glassware
   tax and tip @ $30 per person)
Dance floor 395.00
Tables and chairs 484.00
   (Estimated for 20 tables of 10 persons each @ $8.00
   per table, $1.50 per chair and 3 reception tables)
Table linens *(estimated at $9.00 per linen)* 207.00
Lattice or other room dividers 90.00
Event insurance 100.00
Total cost **$9,926.00**
Estimated cost per person **$50.00**

For the total cost per person, your budget must include all reunion expenses (see sample budget in Chapter 4). If you can still make a ticket price affordable, this option is a creative flair that could enliven your event.

You can reduce costs by just serving finger food and dessert and by supplying your own liquor and soft drink bar. Selling alcoholic drinks will require obtaining a liquor license for the day (if the location doesn't already have one) and hiring professional bartenders. Check with your states' alcoholic beverage control department for appropriate procedures. If you are providing the bar, sell drink tickets so the bartender doesn't have to handle money. Call a few restaurants and hotels for ideas on types and amounts of liquor to have on hand, based on your estimated attendance.

The museum or gallery you select may have a list of recommended bartenders and/or caterers. Compare the prices of the on-site caterer with your own. Get references from any caterer with whom you are not familiar. Ask if you can you test samples.

Resorts/Parks/Campgrounds/Historical Sites

This is a great opportunity for former classmates, families and military buddies to reunite for several days in a casual setting. In addition to room and board, retreats offer various organized activities. Resorts like Montecito Sequoia, in the Northern California Sierra Mountains, is a beautiful location surrounded by wilderness and water and has activities for all ages such as games, hikes, water skiing, archery, tennis, evening concerts or just the indulgence of relaxing among the trees.

If you are planning a one-day event such as a picnic in a local or national park, you'll need a spacious area with picnic tables and barbecue facilities. Picnic areas and baseball diamonds in city-operated parks should be reserved early as they are often already booked far in advance.

Yacht Cruise/Cruise Ships/Steamboats/Houseboats

Have you considered a marina, lake or river cruise reunion? Sea excursions act as a refreshing alternative to the ballroom dinner/dance. Charter a yacht and cruise the waters for several hours or take an extended, week-long cruise along a river or up and down a coast. Contact a travel agent and check the rates on cruises or call some larger cruise liners directly: Princess Cruises, Carnival Cruise Lines, Royal Caribbean Cruise Lines, Holland America and others for their group travel packages. Ask whether they offer supervised activities for children.

The travel section in your newspaper often prints articles and advertises special deals and group discounts. Check the off-season rates. Search under "Cruises" or "Marinas" on the Internet and in the Yellow Pages. Comparison shop. Or, call information and get the numbers for the city's Visitor Center and Convention Bureau.

Steamboats

Have you ever thought of a steamboat trip as a place to reunite? This could be a spirited adventure. Cruises can be as short as 2 days, but the average is 7. With group discounts on airfares, it might not be as expensive as you think. The cruise company will handle deposits, mailings, meals and activities. Entertainment, dancing, lectures, movies and concerts are also provided.

The Delta Queen Steamboat Co. offers 27 different theme cruises year-round; each cruise is designed to invoke the American heritage experience. Three paddlewheel steamboats travel along many U.S. Channels; among them, the Mississippi, Ohio, Tennessee, Cumberland, Arkansas, Illinois, Kanawha, Red and Atchafalaya Rivers and the Intercoastal Waterway. Contact Historic Tours of America 16142 Woodstock Lane,

Huntington Beach, Ca 92647, or call (714) 846-6446.

Houseboats

A reunion on a houseboat cruising down a slow, calm river or lake might be a lot of fun. These generally run through summer months, June - September. Some of the more popular rivers and lakes that offer these rentals are the Sacramento River, Lakes Don Pedro, Oroville and Shasta all in California. You can also try the Mississippi River, Lake Mead in Nevada, Lake Lanier in Georgia, Lake of the Ozarks in Missouri, Lake Meredith in Texas and Lake Powell, Lake Havasu or Lake Mohave in Arizona. Prices range between $1,400 - $1,700 for 3- and 4-day excursions, and between $2,000 - $2,400 for 1 boat on a 7-day trip. Contact Houseboat Association of America in Charleston, South Carolina: (803) 744-6581, e-mail: bobperkins@aol.com. For $3.00 get a listing of all houseboat rental companies in the United States and Canada.

School Gym, Field or Hall

Consider holding a class reunion right at your high school. See if the school will let you use their outdoor grounds, hall or gymnasium. Rent a jukebox. Guests could come dressed in high school garb. Hold a sports event only this time, the teammates are 10, 20, 30 years older! Do this as an inexpensive interim 5-year reunion. Remember though, alcohol may not be allowed on these premises.

Valerie Anderson, chair for her Soldotna High School class reunion in Soldotna, Alaska, planned her 10-year reunion at a local senior citizen center near her high school all the way from her home in Utah. The Center was able to hold all 140 guests comfortably and alcohol could be and was served. The next day, a class/family picnic was held at the local little league fields.

Camps, Conference Centers, Lodges, National Parks

A camp or lodge in a woodsy atmosphere always makes for a relaxed and inexpensive reunion. Nature is very conducive to real connecting. So, plan a day-long outing or a weekend retreat. Arrange activities around meals and evening gatherings being sure to allow ample free time so guests can spend quality time together.

Make sure whatever location is selected meets your groups' needs and has nearby markets for additional meals and snacks.
Tip: Bring your camera!

We reiterate–popular locations need to be reserved well in advance, as long as 2 years prior! Universities, private conference centers, national parks, lodges, camps and youth hostels all have the necessary facilities. Club associations, visitor bureaus and conference centers all have many offerings and services for groups.

Frontier Reunions

An abandoned army fort will create a unique environment for military or family reunions. Preservation and renovation have made these old forts delightfully different. They offer camping, lodging, sporting facilities, biking and hiking trails, tours and site-seeing, stagecoach rides, fishing and hunting, educational and cultural activities and restaurants.

For Midwestern reunions, try Fort Robinson in Nebraska. Reservations for lodging and other facilities are accepted year round, up to one year in advance. Contact: Fort Robinson State Park: (308) 665-2900, P.O. Box 392, Crawford, NE 69339-0392.

If you live in the Northwest, near the Olympic Peninsula, there is Fort Worden in Washington. Book early as they are taking reservations for large groups over a year in advance. Contact: Fort Worden State Park Conference Center, 200 Battery Way, Port Townsend, WA 98368 or call (360) 385-4730.

Additionally, there are many cities in the Midwest not on a Fort that offer rodeos, horseback riding and historic tours in a western ambiance. Cheyenne, Wyoming for example, has such a spot; call 1/800-426-5009 or call a Convention and Visitor Bureau for the city near you.

Multiple Day Combination of Events

Several events over a weekend or a few days, gives more people more time, in more than one environment to really reconnect. It also offers many opportunities for people with scheduling conflicts or financial constraints to attend at least one of the gatherings.

Furthermore, having a casual pre-reunion get-together could be just the trick to ease reunion anxiety. A Sunday brunch, picnic or sports tournament provides a casual setting that won't necessarily mean additional costs, especially if you make it a potluck and bring your own stuff.

If you are selling reunion memorabilia: T-shirts, CD ROMs, photography albums, videos, glassware, caps, mugs or sports bottles, these extra days provide more sales opportunities.

With family members on opposite coasts, two cousins orchestrated their first major family reunion. For the Parziale family's four-day event, Patricia Papanek and Barbara Shapley looked for a place that would accommodate groups, wasn't too expensive and offered privacy. They selected a rustic resort near their Italian family's immigration point back in the early 1900s. It was important that the location be near a hospital (for emergencies), wasn't too tight-quartered and had the potential for organizing entertainment and activities for all ages. They selected *The Benchmark* in Freehold, New York in the Catskills outside Albany. It allowed them to plan many gatherings and meals and had meeting rooms for their own events. They also booked enough people to have the place to themselves. It was a huge success and no one who was there will ever forget.

THE MENU

Food is generally not uppermost on most people's mind when deciding whether or not to attend a reunion. However, we all look forward to the main event and less than wonderful food can make a substantial dent in the overall success of the event.

Select a menu that is in sync with the ambiance you want to create. The sit-down dinner is the classic scenario. Guests are usually given 2 or 3 entree choices. The sit-down dinner confines guests to one small table talking to 2 or 3 people for a good part of the evening. A buffet style dinner affords more variety and guests can mingle more. To avoid long delays waiting in line, suggest that the caterer set up the buffet table so that people can enter from at least two directions. Food stations are ideal for reunions because people are not forced to sit in one place for long periods and crowds are spread out at different locations. Thomas Novic from Wisconsin is a reunion organizer from the 32nd Division Veteran Association. He recommended:

Tip: If you have a sit-down dinner and are offering different entrees, an easy way to identify what each person is having is to put colored tickets or adhesive labels corresponding to their entree choice in their registration packets.

- Under "Alumni Information Screen," go to "Reports," "Name Tags." Select names corresponding to food preferences.
- Print on the designated colored labels and apply to tickets or place cards.

ICE BREAKERS

Ice breakers can be orchestrated, casually planned or presented as an impromptu function. For class reunions, a casual Friday night pre-reunion gathering in the hospitality suite at the hotel sponsoring the dinner dance is an easy event to organize without a whole lot of effort.

Many different emotions come into play in anticipation of attending any reunion and planning a relaxed get-acquainted pre-the-big-event activity will ease those pre-reunion jitters. One family reunion organizer suggests for the first activity, you do something fun. "We asked members to come together in a big circle. Each person told something about themselves that no one else knew about. This turned out to be a exceptional event and we even captured it on video!"

In the 25-year reunion referred to earlier by Joy Malone Dudgeon of Illinois, "*Our 1992 reunion was phenomenal. Money can't buy a better contribution to your memory bank.*" Her multi-day, all school event included registration at the school on a Friday evening, bus tours of the city on Saturday, (a track meet was planned but as bad weather developed, socializing and lunch occurred in a tent and gym), a tree planting ceremony with the city mayor, the school principal and the oldest attending student doing the planting. A dinner/dance took place Saturday night and Sunday morning included an a la carte restaurant brunch. She offered this anecdote:

> A group of sixteen of us got together for an impromptu supper Friday after the arrival/registration gathering at the school. The next day, a long-term friend proclaimed "Nobody has changed very much, isn't it neat? By the way is Roger here?" Well, Roger was sitting directly across the table from him at that supper...

There are many more ideas, books and Websites to explore for additional ideas on reunion locations, products and services. Also, check the resource section at the back of this book. You are only limited by your imagination.

C. STREAMLINE: Maximize Efficiency with Time-saving Techniques

Streamline the time and effort involved by using the tips, tricks and shortcuts, learned the hard way by other reunion planners. This book will also show you how to use a computer program to quickly categorize all your data and how to use the Internet for fast and efficient ways to locate people.

THE COMPUTER PROGRAM

We have included suggestions throughout this book on how to best utilize the computer program that has been designed to especially accompany this book. Computer icons appear when the program's usage is recommended.

When searching for people and entering guest information, the following lists will help organize your data.

Lists
- All Invited Guests
- All Attending
- Not Attending
- Located
- Not Located
- Located, Responded

- Located, Not Responded
- Responded
- Tickets Paid
- Purchased Items

Create lists under each of these headings. Keep careful records and duplicate copies of all names, addresses, phone numbers. Reports can be viewed either alphabetically (using women's maiden and married names) or by area code.

Mailings are made much easier because our program prints hundreds of address labels in just a few minutes using any listing mentioned above or for individually selected names. If a lot of guests will be traveling from long distances, check the *"Out-of-Towners"* box in the "Alumni Information Screen" for labels and reports relevant to them. This function is helpful in notifying guests of special group travel packages and discounts.

Keep track of your attendance statistics to see the percentage of guests invited, responded and located.   The program breaks the information down according to total, male/female attendees.

This computer program will be invaluable in assembling your reunion memory album. Everyone attending will get a roster with names, addresses, phone numbers and E-mail addresses.

Budget Assistance

The way to feel totally confident you won't run out of money is to set up a detailed budget. The program will help you make calculations based on the existing and anticipated financial situations. You can test different ticket prices based on various expense scenarios.

- Estimated expenses
- Estimated receipts
- Anticipated net balance

Additional Features
- Prints invitations
- Makes name tags

▸ Use the "Comment" section to enter RSVPs and interest level. This is very useful for future phone drives.

▸ When everything is organized on one computer disk, you won't have to reinvent the wheel for each subsequent reunion

▸ Create a database of responses from questionnaires you have send out. This is helpful for program awards. (See Chapters 9 and 10 for award categories.)

Purchase *"The Complete Reunion Planner"* program by completing and sending in the order form on the last page of this book or directly from our Website.

SEARCHING FOR PEOPLE

This portion of planning a reunion takes the most effort and the longest time. Finding and notifying people is the essence of pulling off your reunion. While it can be the most tedious part, it can also be the most rewarding. During the year before our reunion, I enjoyed wonderful "mini reunions" and conversations with alumni that I would never have had the opportunity for during the shorter events. Plus, I got to connect with all of the people who weren't able to come to the reunion.

Some people never bother to find out about reunions and hope someone will find and contact **them.** As hard as it is to find people, and as much as people do want to attend, so many of us fail to make that simple phone call to their alma mater/school/military base to find out if a reunion is being planned. Then, we're thrilled when someone finds us!

More and more, universities and colleges are thinking of ways to keep in constant touch with alumni. According to the May 15, 1997 issue of the Wall Street Journal, staying connected electronically is the way to go. The paper reported that Harvard Business School assigns E-mail addresses to all 66,000 alumni. This benefits the school and the alumni. Indeed, this is the future. It will be much easier for high schools, families and military veterans to easily and inexpensively have ongoing communication regardless of how far or how often people move.

Where to Start

According to research, the greatest percentage of people still live within 50 miles of where they grew up. So, you can start with local area phone directories. You will have a distinct advantage in locating people if you know the first, middle and last names and/or a relative's name.

When you have a list of twenty Bill Smiths to call from phone books or the Internet, don't get discouraged. The last one may be a relative or the real person. As for all those wrong numbers, once you explain to them the reason for your call, people are generally happy you're not trying to sell them something and don't mind the interruption.

Based on responses from the survey from our first edition of *The Reunion Planner*, most alumni were located from previous reunion lists, local phone books, and personal contacts. Respondents like the Jentinks from Eagan, Minnesota found computerized programs for the entire United States at their local library.

STAY ORGANIZED BY KEEPING LISTS

The *Checklist* that immediately follows this chapter is a handy reminder of all conceivable tasks. Circle the ones that pertain to you. Make several copies of this list, highlight specific tasks and distribute to each volunteer. This way, each person has his/her own to-do list and can check off the items as they're completed.

It will help to keep notes, like the suggested chart below, on potential reunion locations and what follow up needs to take place.

Potential Reunion Sites

Location and Contact Person	Phone	Price

Follow Up	Date to call back	Called Back?

Additional Comments: _____

_____

_____

_____

Checklist

☐ Design a slide show
☐ Choose a photographer
☐ Plan a picnic
☐ Open a bank account
☐ Make files and organize the paperwork

9 Months Before the Reunion

Create an Ambiance 6
☐ Develop a social action project
☐ Create and order mementos and souvenirs
    ☐ memory album or other booklet
    ☐ name tags
☐ Create tickets and acknowledgment postcards
☐ Work on genealogy charts and family history book
☐ Hire videographer or oral history preparer
☐ Edit and organize personal histories, cookbook, photographs, videos for reunion handout or display
☐ Update address list
☐ Continue the people search

Getting People There 7
☐ Meet regularly to make phone calls
☐ Invite special guests
☐ Prepare and send second mailer

6 Months Before the Reunion

Reunion Decor 8
☐ Plan decorations, displays and centerpieces
☐ Edit personal histories, update address list
☐ Continue the phone drive
☐ Find T-shirt vendor
☐ Order reunion mementos
☐ Order souvenirs, awards and door prizes
☐ Order banner
☐ Order napkins, pens and other give-a-ways

3 Months Before the Reunion

Countdown **11**
- ☐ Update address list, edit histories, continue phone drive
- ☐ Order banner
- ☐ Get event insurance
- ☐ Order T-shirts
- ☐ Rent a dance floor
- ☐ Recruit registration desk workers
- ☐ Send reminder notices
- ☐ Start making name tags
- ☐ Make table centerpieces
- ☐ Prepare photo collage, signs and door prize coupons
- ☐ Prepare a printed program
- ☐ Draft oral program notes and announcements

1 Month Before the Reunion
- ☐ Edit personal histories, update address list, continue name tags and phone drive
- ☐ Send reminder postcards
- ☐ Select preliminary award winners
- ☐ Make signs for registration area

2 Weeks Before the Reunion

Final Arrangements **12**
- ☐ Mail tickets
- ☐ Verify event attendance, prepare list of paid guests
- ☐ Verify attendance of registration desk workers
- ☐ Check floral arrangements
- ☐ Confirm details with entertainer, videographer, photographer and other vendors
- ☐ Verify attendance and/or arrange accommodations, if necessary, for invited guests
- ☐ Finalize program announcements and award winners
- ☐ Verify delivery of donated door prizes
- ☐ Proof memory album draft or other handout and give artwork to printer

1 Week Before the Reunion

☐ Prepare final list of paid attendees
☐ Prepare registration packets
    ☐ pre-paid ticket holders
    ☐ will call
☐ Make signs for registration tables
☐ Give meal count to caterer and final payment to facility
☐ Verify room set up and equipment arrangements with the banquet manager
☐ Create contingency plan

The Reunion Event

It's Reunion Time **13**
☐ Bring reunion day checklist
☐ Retrieve supplies at end of reunion

Aftermath **14**
☐ Finalize photo book and send to photographer
☐ Send memory albums and other hand-outs to those who paid but did not attend reunion events
☐ Send prepared documents to individual purchasers
☐ Send thank you notes
☐ Send follow-up letter
☐ Send donation to school, alumni association or other preferred charity
☐ Close bank account once all checks have cleared
☐ Store reunion supplies in convenient location
☐ Complete and E-mail, send or fax in Reunion Survey to Goodman Lauren Publishing. Or, complete survey on Website: *www.reunionplanner.com/survey*

Stay Up to Date on Reunion Planning **15**
☐ Keep the ambiance alive by maintaining a regular newsletter
☐ Hold follow up committee meeting to discuss reunion successes and pitfalls
☐ Check Website for updates

3

Finding People on the Internet
How the Internet Can Help Promote
a Successful Reunion

These days, the Internet has become the most convenient resource for finding anything. With between 20 and 30 million people surfing the Internet, it has made the task of finding people and announcing reunions easier, quicker and broader in scope. The Internet offers instantaneous information and access to phone directories all over the world. It is an impressive forum for anyone searching for information on reunions. New Websites are appearing daily, as schools, military organizations, religious groups and every organization under the sun are jumping on the Internet.

To get connected, you need a computer, a modem, an Internet Service Provider (ISP) and an Internet Browser. There are many ISPs to choose from – AOL, Earthlink, Pacbell, etc. – which simply give your computer a way to connect to the Internet through your telephone lines.

Your set up kit will include lots of information about the Internet. Your library, bookstore and phone company offer many excellent guides explaining its history and operation. If you want hands on instruction, computer and Internet classes abound at junior colleges and night classes at high schools. We applaud those of you who are already part of the global community on the NET, or plan to be there soon.

Once you're connected, your Internet Browser (AOL, Netscape Navigator, Microsoft Internet Explorer, etc.) will have access to the millions of search engines (Internet locater vehicles) of people finding resources. They update these international phone directories frequently, some more than others. So you should hunt through several search engines to maximize your results. Use all the free search devices before you decide to pay for any locator assistance.

INTERNET BASICS

First, check to see if your school, religious organization, military association or other group you are reuniting has a URL (Uniform Resource Locator) or Website. A URL is an electronic address for web pages. It's the code that identifies where a particular site can be found. Most sites begin with **"http://www."** Http:// is often treated as a given and left out of published addresses and with some browsers, unnecessary. Some sites now leave out the **"www"** in their address.

As an increasingly popular vehicle for public relations, advertising, fundraising, personal Websites and general information, the Internet has hundreds of new sites opening every day. To simplify your search, we've selected sites that, as of this printing, we thought were the most effective.

As you scan various sites, you'll discover more links to related sites providing even more direction for finding people. The following suggestions should get you started.

There are many search engines that are national white page phone directories and can be reached by simply looking up people-finding resources through your Internet browser. For example, AOL uses *Switchboard* as their locator service (as of this printing) but you can directly access Switchboard at their Website: *http://www.switchboard.com.*

Some sites are more current than others, so experiment with various search engines. Look for people-finding resources at the standard search engine sites including: Yahoo, Lycos, AltaVista, Excite, Infoseek, WebCrawler and the list goes on. Find them through your Internet service provider. Each can be accessed by typing *www.* before and *.com* after their name. Addresses ending in *.com* represent a commercial entity, *.edu* is an educational institution and *.org* depicts a nonprofit organization.

There are many sites that specialize in people finding resources such as Switchboard, Four11, WhoWhere, Bigfoot, pc411, ATT, DatabaseAmerica and Infospace. Some sites find names, addresses, business addresses and E-mail addresses. IAF.NET (Internet Address Finder) has a sizable list of E-mail names and addresses of people who have signed up with their service. All these can be accessed beginning with ***http://www.*** and ending with ***.com/*** leaving no spaces between words.

A group site called ***http://www.555-1212.com*** links Infospace, Four11, Switchboard and DatabaseAmerica and has several choices such as "qwikfill" that searches all these search engines at once. It also has "reverse look-up" where they connect a name and address to a given phone number. It does not require a city or state to search, so you can find long-lost cousin Betty, no matter where she is, provided she does not have an unlisted number. Another group site links Yahoo!, WhoWhere, Switchboard, Four11, Infospace, pc411 and Worldpages called ***http://www.theultimates.com.***

Some sites want you to join and pay membership fees. Others offer some services free and additional services for members. I was very successful using a variety of search locators without paying any membership fees.

CLASS REUNION SITES

Ever more school alumni associations have Websites and/or listings of whom to contact for information. Look for the sites that specialize in helping people find lost classmates, family and friends.

▸ *http://www.classmates.com*
A Website specifically designed to find high school alumni is called Classmates™. It provides a registry of people who have listed their names and E-mail addresses for hundreds of high schools all

over the world. They reportedly have more than 300 overseas school listings (as of this writing). If you are the contact for your reunion, they will list you as the "reunion contact" and you will receive updates on new registrants bimonthly, even after your reunion. At a $20 fee for three years, alumni in search of a contact can access and send e-mails to registrants when they become paid members.

Reunion-based Websites encourage alumni to enter their school reunion notices.

▸ **http://www.bbhq.com**
This site is devoted to baby boomers (those born from 1946 - 1964). It has a segment called *Reunion Central* which offers reunion planners a spot to announce their reunions and link a detailed message on the bulletin board and a baby boomer registry. For a fee, they will design a Web page for your school with reunion information that your alumni can access and send E-mail to, which will be forwarded to you. They will even maintain the site until your next reunion for another fee.

▸ **http://www.alumni.net**
This site is a worldwide alumni registry that links you to alumni that have signed up on this site. Pick your country, state, city and high school. Scroll to your graduation year and check for alumni that have registered. You can send E-mail messages to anyone listed. It is a location where alumni who want to be found can be contacted. Whenever someone registers on this site, automatic bimonthly updates are E-mailed to the reunion contact. It's a great resource for planners.

▸ **http://www.gemneye.com/reunions/reunions.html**
A Website called **Reunions R Us** was initiated by a Pasadena high school alum in California while searching for fellow classmates. He developed a Website for high school reunions throughout the United States. It lists upcoming and ongoing reunion events at no charge. They list the schools alphabetically within each state. The site invites you to link your reunion or alumni organizing committee too.

Many locator sites link people based on similar backgrounds and interests, which often include high schools, colleges, professional affiliations and hobbies. This helps to narrow the scope of your search. List your reunion information with these sites. If you don't want to mention your home address on the Internet, use an office address or your high school's. Call occasionally to remind the school to forward the information to you.

MILITARY SEARCH SITES

There also are many military reunion/alumni sites on the Web both in the United States and overseas. There is an organization for military brats (offspring of the U.S. military stationed overseas) called "Overseas Brats." This organization is dedicated to preserving the heritage and experiences of students and educators of American families stationed overseas.

They are hosting an all-overseas reunion August 5-8, 1999 in Grapevine, Texas. Their Website has areas of interest and an address at which you can leave messages: *http://www.vni.net/~mcl/osb/osbmain.htm.* For more details, call Joe Condrill, President, at (201) 349-1394 or E-mail him at obpres@aol.com or call Linda Irvine, (602) 935-3939.

▶ *http://www.lynxu.com*
▶ *http://www.military-brats.com*

Military Brats Online is a network of overseas high school alumni associations. Register or look for alumni whether you attended stateside or overseas schools:

You can also access and leave messages for the Overseas Brats section in AOL's "Military City Online" (MCO) by typing MCO only via the provider AOL. In the American section of the military/veterans club on AOL, look in "Military Brats."

American OverSeas Historical Society, AOSHS, is planning to build a museum replete with up-to-date lists and archives and a Visitors Center dedicated to those who attended American Overseas Schools around the world. Planned for the year 2000, the museum, besides preserving their history, will be a location to contact lost alumni and faculty. Dr. Tom Drysdale, founder of AOSHS, can be reached at (602) 935-3939 or OverseasSchools@juno.com.

▶ *http://www.militarycity.com*
   A large site (with free and subscription areas) that includes a search engine for veterans and a public bulletin board. They invite all current service members, retirees and veterans of the United States Armed Forces to register.

▶ *http://members.aol.com/veterans/index.html*
   This is another veterans' page. It has more than 17 million military/veteran registrations in their locator database.

▶ *http://www.the-seeker.com/military.htm*
   A military search page that allows you to post who you're looking for or be notified when anyone is trying to find you.

▶ *http://www.vietvet.org*
   This site has a Lost and Found locator for Vietnam veterans and friends of vets looking for each other. Anyone can post searches. *http:/grunt.space.swri.edu* is the Vietnam Veterans home page that has a list of veterans' groups and a place to post searches. It announces unit reunions, prints newsletters and lists points of contacts. Remember to register your reunion information at both sites! The Vietnam Veterans' memorial wall page can be accessed at: *http://www.thewall-usa.com.* It lists veterans killed in the war.

▶ *http://www.koreanwar.org*
   This site is the home page for Korean War veterans. While it does not have listings for veterans who are still living, it has a casualty list of veterans, killed or missing in action. The site also has a list of reunions.
   A new search organization called Registry of American Veterans (ROAV), gathers information from veterans, entering their name, residence, military units and era served. Those who sign up with the Registry receive an annual printout of the veterans in ROAV's database listed according to who served in the same unit and time, including current addresses and phone numbers.
   Look for any current armed service personnel through one of the many military sites and home pages for each branch of the military service. Add your own listing in the military service branch with which you're associated.

FAMILY RESEARCH SITES

▸ *http://lds.org*
▸ *http://www2.kbyu.org/ancestors*
▸ *http://www.ysite.com/lds.htm*

The Church of Jesus Christ of Latter-day Saints (LDS) is by far the largest and most comprehensive resource in the world for researching family histories, genealogical research and family trees.

Their well known Family History Library in Salt Lake City, Utah is connected to their many Family History Centers, FHC, in each state and throughout the world. Each has a collection of databases on CD-ROM called FamilySearch ™, which lists millions of names of people who have had previous research done. They use a variety of original records on CD-ROM and microfiche. Anyone can access this information free. (Chapter 10 has details on what's out there.) As of this writing, the FHCs do not have direct Internet access to family search engines, but keep checking their Website–that could change.

All these sites have links to, and information on, similar topics. Check out the related Websites they suggest.

▸ *http://www.ancestry.com/ancestry/search.asp*

For family tree searches, this ancestry Web page contains a variety of databases (on-line public records) including immigration, military, census, court/probate deeds, land and vital records (birth, marriage, death, etc.). You can perform an ancestral global search for relatives still living though you might only know a few details on the person you're trying to find. For those who have passed on, you can look through the social security death index. After **ancestry.com** put **/ssdi/advanced.htm.** They also have a world tree which is a free database of family files submitted by family history enthusiasts all over the world.

▸ *http://rro.everton.com/ssmdi.html.*

The site for "Everton's On-Line Search," based in Logan, Utah, holds the addresses of more than 60 million records. By enlarging a surname and first name, you'll get birth and death dates, the person's last place of residence and their social security number as reported to the Social Security Administration from 1962 to 1993. There's more on this Center and what it offers in Chapter 10.

Many families have established their own Internet sites with genealogy pages and ongoing family reunion information and communications. Look at these sites for ideas on starting your own Internet family resource center.

▸ *http://www.familytreemaker.com*
Broderbund Software, Inc., a company that specializes in family tree software, has a free family finder on their site. It automatically searches through genealogy pages, indexes and records all across the Internet. They advertise their software which explores even more search vehicles and public records. They are linked to just about every genealogy site on the Internet. You can go directly to their search section: *http://www.familytreemaker.com/ifftop.html*.

▸ *http://www.teleport.com/~binder/famtree.shtml*
A genealogy publication with a Scottish bent based out of Moultrie, Georgia puts out a bimonthly newsletter called "The Family Tree" with news from the Ellen Payne Odam Genealogy Library (check Resources for address). Besides listing your own family reunion, you can read their articles and book reviews. You'll find useful information on genealogy plus they're a great resource for finding services and materials for a variety of cultures.

▸ *http://www.reunionsmag.com/reunions_list.html*
A magazine that specializes in all reunions has a Web page that announces your military, family or class reunion both on their site and in their magazine. *Reunions Magazine* is a quarterly publication and each issue is packed with ideas, stories and articles geared to reunion organizers. If you want your reunion announced in their magazine, they require six months advance notification. Quicker yet, visit their Website to add your reunion or link your Website.

▸ *http://www.reunited.com*
Based in Fort Lauderdale, Florida, this site allows you to search for high school, military or family reunions. Experienced reunion

committees and planners announce their event on many bulletin boards. List your reunion on their board.

▸ *http://www.reunions.com*
Based in Tampa, Florida, this is the National Association of Reunion Managers (NARM). Besides offering school reunion committees a wide membership of professional planners throughout the United States, committees can list announcements for their upcoming events for alumni seeking reunion information. Keep checking our Webpage: *http://www.reunionplanner.com* and other reunion sites for updates on new sites, ideas and information. Register and announce your reunion in as many reunion Internet sites as possible to get the word out to the widest possible audience. With its increasing popularity, the Internet is the ideal way to announce your reunion. It's especially important when there is no longer a reunion home base.

GENERAL SITES AND RELATED INFORMATION

▸ *http://lawyers.martindale.com/marhub.*
Find anyone whoever practiced law in the US. Just provide a name to Martin-Hubbell® Lawyer Locator™. Another lawyer locator is: *http://www.unilegal.com/links.htm.*

▸ *http://ama-assn.org*
This is the home page for the American Medical Association. Under "Doctor Finder" you can search by physician name or medical specialty. You must include the state. It will give you the doctor's full name, state, city and zip code, whether they're an AMA member or not.

▸ *http://www.usps.gov*
If you input in the city and state, the US Postal Service will give you zip code information. Inversely, if you list the zip code, it finds the corresponding city and state. You'll be given the four digit extension of an organization's address when you enter the business name.

▸ *http://www.reunionregistry.com*
A site with a different slant! It's the only entirely free site of its kind. Here, you can register yourself or see whether anyone else is looking for you.

Again, these are sites offering free Internet searches. There are many more that will conduct searches for fees.

MORE PEOPLE-FINDING RESOURCES

1. Check through local and outlying area telephone books. Phone books and zip code directories for all of the United States are available in the larger public libraries.

2. Request referrals during phone drives.

3. Send *Missing Persons* lists in all mailings.

4. Use parents' addresses. If you're lucky enough to have parents' first names, that's even better.

5. Contact your alumni association and see if you can place no-cost ads in their newsletters and mailings.

6. Create public service announcements (PSAs), and air them on local radio stations. There are no fees for PSAs.

7. Many local newspapers also offer a section for free reunion announcements.

8. Church bulletins, alumni association newsletters, genealogy society newsletters or military magazines also have a section listing upcoming reunions.

9. There are usually one or two family members that have will have a "library" of history/addresses/information for your family.

10. The County Assessor's office property tax records. You can search through an alphabetical listing of properties which includes names and addresses free.

11. The County Registrar of Voters is also free. They list registered voters with names, addresses, birthdates and sometimes phone numbers.

12. State Departments of Motor Vehicles (DMVs) have search services for a minimum fee per name. This access is not available in many states.

13. County Marriage License Bureaus are helpful for finding women's married names.

14. County Hall of Records has public birth records. They record parents' full names and addresses with the child's name.

15. Search through university alumni records and college associations as sorority and fraternity lists.

16. Reunion committees of bordering class years might have relatives of people you are looking for.

In all likelihood, the fastest and most economical method for finding people is through the Internet. Nevertheless, you only have so much time to commit to these efforts. The core of reunion planning should be on making personal phone calls to get people excited about attending the reunion.

For updates on new people-finding sites, visit our Website at *http://www.reunionplanner.com.* Besides finding new people-finders and related reunion sites, we offer a forum to planners so they can share their experiences including talking about what works and what doesn't. We have the latest tools and tips on reunion planning services. Planners have the ability to create their own Website. Reunion products and services are also offered to insure your reunion is the event not to be missed.

MORE INTERNET SITES

4
Create a Budget
To Balance, You Must Budget

It is good practice to set up a budget to ensure the financial success of any event. For a reunion, it not only is good practice, it is essential for selecting a ticket price and determining the kind of event you can afford.

GOAL SETTING

Estimate your preliminary cost projections using the Budget Worksheet. The Sample Worksheet will help you create a preliminary budget. Make several copies of this page, and use a pencil, as you will likely be making changes. By experimenting with different ticket prices and along with an estimated turnout, decide what your limit on expenses is since you cannot exceed estimated revenues. Closer to the date of the reunion, a final budget should be prepared. After the event, a closeout budget must be completed to verify your estimates and financial records. A final, actual budget will be very helpful for the next reunion.

- Under Budget Data, enter assumptions and prepare an estimated budget.
- Move the cursor to Actual Budget and enter correct amounts as expenses are incurred.

ASSUMPTIONS

Total Guests
Enter the amount of total, potential guests.

Estimated Turnout
Be conservative. In determining your expected attendance, a slight underestimation of guests is a safer bet for choosing what size banquet room to book. A restaurant or hotel can always add a few more tables if more people show up, but a large room with few tables is . . . well, not very cozy. Various factors will affect attendance such as the time between reunions. The more frequently-held reunions will experience less attendance.

For more assistance, contact other reunion coordinators. Catering managers at large hotels or restaurants will be helpful too. Experience is always a reliable resource. In the sample budget, for a 20-year reunion, the total potential guest list was multiplied by 40%. This included spouses.

A per-unit estimated turnout will be required for deciding how many individual items are needed. Use this figure when only one item as T-shirts, programs or photo books, per classmate or family unit is necessary. It is safe to assume, for example, that each family will share one cookbook. In the sample budget, 65% of the estimated turnout (130) was estimated.

SAMPLE BUDGET

ASSUMPTIONS	
Total Membership	500
Estimated Turnout (membership plus guests @ 40%)	200
Estimated Turnout (membership only @ 65%)	130
Tables Required (10 people per table)	20

ESTIMATED EXPENSES

Item	Unit Cost	Item	Per Unit	Total Cst.
Meal (Incl. tax & tip)	$32.50	person	200	$6,500
Entertainment	$650.00		1	$650
Postage	$0.32	envelope	950	$286
Printing/copying	$200.00		1	$200
Name tags	$1.00	member	130	$130
Centerpieces	$18.00	table	20	$360
Balloons/decorations	$600.00		1	$600
Photo Album	$10.00	member	130	$1,300
Directory	$3.00	member	130	$390
Door prizes/awards	$10.00	prize	10	$100
Committee gifts	$10.00	person	8	$80
Programs	$1.50	member	130	$195
Comp. meals	$30.00	person	4	$120
A/V equipment	$300.00		1	$300
Banner	$100.00		1	$100
Insurance	$100.00		1	$100
Miscellaneous	$100.00		1	$100

TOTAL EXPENSES   **$11,511**

ESTIMATED REVENUES

Item	Unit Amt.	Item	Per Unit	Total
Ticket sales	$60.00	person	200	$12,000
Reunion Item sales	$5.00	item	50	$250
Advertising	$20.00	ad	10	$200
Sponsors				
Other				

TOTAL REVENUES   **$12,450**

    BALANCE   **$939**

COST PER PERSON   **$58**

(Cost per person represents expenses divided by estimated
attendance and rounded up.)

BUDGET WORKSHEET

ASSUMPTIONS	
Total Membership	
Estimated Turnout (membership plus guests @ 40%)	
Estimated Turnout (membership only @ 65%)	
Tables Required (10 people per table)	

ESTIMATED EXPENSES

Item	Unit Cost	Item	Per Unit	Total Cst.
Meal (Incl. tax & tip)		person		
Entertainment				
Postage		envelope		
Printing/copying				
Name tags		member		
Centerpieces		table		
Balloons/decorations				
Photo Album		member		
Programs		member		
Door prizes/awards		prize		
Miscellaneous				

TOTAL EXPENSES $_____

ESTIMATED REVENUES

Item	Unit Amt.	Item	Per Unit	Total
Ticket sales		person		

TOTAL REVENUES $_____

BALANCE $_____

COST PER PERSON $_____

Tables Required

Divide the expected turnout by 10. This is a standard number of seats per table. This will be necessary in estimating how many centerpieces and table linens will be required.

EXPENSES

Room Rental, Meal Costs and Entertainment

If you chose a hotel or restaurant, the dance floor, tables and chairs, utensils, table linens, waiters and bartenders (above a minimum in bar sales) are included in the total per-person cost. However, if you select a facility that requires you to rent these items, do not forget to add these costs to your expenses.

Once the place and the menu are chosen, you've determined the most important and largest reunion expense. (Be sure to include tax and tip in the total cost per person.) The cost of entertainment can be calculated by surveying professional disc jockeys (DJs). In our example, $650 was used as an average cost for hiring a DJ in the Los Angeles area for four hours.

Printing, Copying and Postage

Printing and copying costs, including stationery, envelopes, postcards, name tags, programs and tickets can be configured by estimating the number of mailings and your expected turnout. Postage costs in our example were based on our class size of 500, with three mailings, as follows:

1. A 500-piece mailing to the entire group.
2. A 300-piece second mailing. This reduced amount assumes that a third of the envelopes in the first mailer will be returned with incorrect or unforwardable addresses.
3. 150 reminder postcards.

Under this scenario, at 32¢ for first class postage and 20¢ per postcard, postage costs total/$286.

Photo Album/Memory Book
    The costs of these items will be based on who is doing the most work. For example, a lot can be saved on a memory album if volunteers put forth most of the effort leaving only printing costs. A reunion photo book can range between $8 and $30 depending whether it's done in black and white or color. Call other reunion photographers for quotations.

Table Centerpieces
    For live floral arrangements, call any florist for their price list. Creating your own centerpieces can be more economical. Helium balloons are popular and festive. There are many balloon companies that cater large events and have designers who can suggest arrangements based on your budget. Party stores also sell balloons and rent helium tanks. Once final selections are made, the true costs for these items can replace the estimated ones. The budget can then be reevaluated and, if necessary, adjusted.

Decorations
    Other decorations, such as a banner, posters, more balloons, photo displays, etc., can be calculated by calling stationery stores and graphic design studios. Of course, members of your committee can create your own.

Miscellaneous
    T-shirts, door prizes, name tags, audio/visual equipment, programs, thank you gifts, insurance, parking fees and other miscellaneous costs should be included in the preliminary budget. If anything is donated like door prizes, printing costs, stationery supplies or auction items, these estimated expenses can be reduced or eliminated in your final budget. A category for all the little extras is judged at 2 to 3 percent of the total budget. Such charges might include bank account fees, reimbursements for phone calls, parking costs, committee meeting snacks and hotel/entertainment tips.

Total Expenses
    In the sample budget, total expenses are estimated at $11,511 or about $58 per person.

REVENUES

The ticket price must cover all estimated expenses. Remember to consider a price that most people would consider affordable. In our example, we chose $60 per person anticipating that this was both the maximum we could charge and the minimum we needed to include the features we envisioned.

Total Revenues

The figure for total revenues will be based mainly on ticket receipts. Think of proceeds from other sales such as T-shirts and photo books as icing on the cake. There will be additional income from higher ticket prices for latecomers paying at the door. However, it is recommended that you use one base ticket price when estimating revenues from ticket sales.

Advertising income from business card sales @ $20 an ad could generate $200 if 10 people send in cards. If you create your own business directory with ads, be sure to include that item in the expense column. For example, $3 per book for 130 people costs $390. Placing business card ads in your photo book/memory album is more economical. A final decision on preparing a directory can be based on the number of ads sold. This additional revenue is uncertain, so be conservative in your estimate.

<u>Balancing the Budget.</u> Remember, revenues from ticket sales must cover all expenses.

SELECT A TICKET PRICE

Costs can be adjusted or eliminated, however, you must remember that once a ticket price has been selected, this will be a cap for determining revenues. The surplus meant we could afford more elaborate centerpieces, a more professional looking memory album or a larger charitable donation.

RAISING ADDITIONAL CASH

Maintaining a positive ending balance is the ideal goal. However, as you get closer to the reunion, and you may be short on cash, there are many ways to raise additional funds. Please don't ask for donations at the reunion! This is bad management and a negative approach. Further, attendees will likely be reluctant to contribute at this point having spent so much just to get to the reunion.

First, refer to Chapter 2 for early fundraising ideas. Then, look for expenses that can be reduced or eliminated. Listed below are additional suggestions that are simple and can be put together on short notice.

Business Card Directory

Include a section in your photo book or memory album for business cards and charge $15 - $20 per card. A variation on the theme would be to create a business directory as a handout at the reunion. Charge a small fee such as $5 per entry and list the names, addresses and phone numbers in an 8½" x 11" format. If some people want to include a full business card, charge more. A more elaborate presentation would be to include a yearbook or family picture. Be sure to thank contributors and encourage patronage of their businesses.

Raffles

A relatively easy and inexpensive fall-back for last minute fundraising appeals is to hold a raffle.

▸ A class yearbook or family heirloom will bring in a lot of money at the last minute. Many alumni have lost their yearbooks and would pay big bucks to get one back, even without the original autographs. In fact, a reunion is the perfect place to update those autographs or get some that were missed the first time around. Many would consider it the ideal opportunity and some may even feel it has more value.

▸ Purchase disposable cameras in bulk and sell them at a higher price at the registration desk. Many attendees will not have thought to bring cameras and welcome the opportunity to buy one.

▸ Specialty bottles of wine. (Examples on page 124).

▸ Donations from local businesses such as dinner for two at an enjoyable restaurant, tickets to a theatrical event, museum membership, theme park admission, movie tickets or gift certificate at any local store. Charge a modest amount such as $1 per raffle ticket. Ask someone who has a "sales personality" in your committee network to sell raffle tickets at the check-in table and ask the DJ to announce the raffle at dinner. Select the winner during the program.

Laurie Zack from Lansing, Michigan was planning her 30-year high school reunion. She wrote us that her 10-year-old daughter wanted to help so she had her sell raffle tickets at the door. While it was her husband who handled the money, it was her daughter's charming personality that produced more than $200 in raffle ticket sales.

Many establishments make donations to nonprofit organizations. While you don't have to file for nonprofit status, your community businesses might be sympathetic toward your event. Simply make a few phone calls and offer free advertising in your memory album, newsletter, mailing or other display at the reunion.

Reunion Items for Sale

Charge a few dollars extra for items being sold at the reunion such as T-shirts, videos, cookbooks, photo albums, etc. If a vendor is handling sales, ask a friend or family member to help with cataloging the purchases.

Flower Baskets /Table Centerpieces

Buy terra cotta pots and ask an artistic person you know to paint reunion-related designs on them. Add real plants. Use them as table centerpieces. Announce the winners during the evening program. Sell as silent auction items or charge a flat fee, e.g., $20-$25 each and sell them during the social hour.

If you are working with professional planners, and need additional funds to cover an expense that isn't in their "packaged deal," work out an arrangement where they charge a few dollars extra per ticket and reimburse the committee the overage.

Chapter 9 has more fundraising ideas for family and military reunions.

THE COMPUTER BUDGET REPORT

If you have *The Complete Reunion Planner* computer software, input assumptions for all expenses and revenues. Then try different budget scenarios. After entering estimated expenses, adjust costs or the ticket price until a positive ending balance is achieved.

With this report, you can reconcile the monthly bank statement. As actual expense dollars become known, this information can be entered into your estimated budget. Slowly, you'll see a more accurate appraisal of your financial situation. As people send in money for tickets or other items, you will be better able to estimate how many items (T-shirts, photo books or other favors) to order.

9 Months
Before the Reunion

5
The Foundation
In Other Words,
Basic Building Blocks

Make the most out of committee meetings. If you are well prepared, you can accomplish a lot. As chairperson, you should assess each individual's abilities and willingness to perform. Before each subsequent meeting send, fax or E-mail meeting notices. Include an agenda of what is to be accomplished and the estimated meeting length. (See sample meeting notice in Chapter 2.) Based on goals to be met, delegate tasks.

GETTING THE WORD OUT
Letting everyone know very soon that a reunion is in the works greatly increases your attendance potential. Over the past three months as addresses are being updated, the master list should be more current. If envelopes need to be hand addressed, as opposed to any number of computer programs which print out labels in a jiffy, ask volunteers to address the envelopes prior coming to the meeting. If you are using labels, purchase a box of no less than 100

sheets. Avery labels and other brands are sold in a variety of sizes per page. To save money, buy office supplies as staples, envelopes, paper and the like, in stores that sell in bulk.

■ **Print address labels.**
■ **Print two sets of return address labels; one for the included reply envelopes and one as return addresses for the main envelopes (unless envelopes are preprinted).**

Send the first announcement to everyone. Use whatever addresses they know. For high school reunions, you will find that many parents still have the same address and can pass along reunion information to their children.

Include the statement **"Change Service Requested"** somewhere on the outside of the envelope. If you are mailing bulk rate, the fee for return service with new address or reason for non-delivery is the current first class single rate or 33¢ per piece as of 1999. If mail sent first class is received within a forwarding time frame, letters will be returned to the sender with the corrected address.

Several benefits will be achieved from this early mailing:

▸ reservations with some early needed cash

▸ personal histories for the memory album

▸ pictures for the family history album, video or display

▸ addresses of yet more potential attendees

▸ early word-of-mouth

▸ additional volunteers to help with planning

▸ early, discounted airline fares or group rate hotel arrangements

CONTENTS OF THE FIRST MAILING

The Announcement

Design the invitation. If you have access to a computer, experiment with different fonts and graphics. We've seen wonderfully creative invitations. If you don't have a computer, use press-on letters, available in stationery stores. There's a wealth of paper choices – from recycled to day-glo. If possible, create a new logo or use the school's mascot for maximum nostalgic effect. If the reunion particulars are known at this time, define them.

- **Create the reunion announcement.**

- **Prepare a questionnaire or survey.**

Design the Invitation

► Date, place, length and approximate starting time.

► Cost per person or payment request.

► If you have chosen the reunion location and have the ticket price, announce it in this mailer. You do want to generate early payments. Coming up with a ticket price will be easier once you've figured out a budget, even if it's still an estimate. Another way to encourage early reservations is to designate cutoff dates for lower priced tickets. Be sure to suggest **to whom to make out the check.**

▸ Preliminary agenda or itinerary of events.

▸ Payment acknowledgment. In your announcement, show how ticket payments will be acknowledged, i.e., "Your canceled check is your receipt," "Tickets will be held at the door." Or, "An acknowledgment postcard will be mailed upon receipt of your check," "Tickets will be mailed approximately two weeks before the event."

▸ Missing persons list.

▸ Reservation form/questionnaire.

▸ Overnight accommodations including early bird prices.

▸ Any reunion items sale with price list.

▸ Request for old pictures, 8 millimeter film transferred to video or slides for memorabilia display or other memento.

▸ Names and phone numbers of whom to contact with questions.

Personal Data
As much personal data as possible:

▸ Last name, a maiden name, nickname and first name or, the name you used when we knew you

▸ Number of attendees in party

▸ Address, City, State and Zip

▸ E-mail address

▸ Home and business phone numbers

▸ Spouse or guest's name

▸ Location and/or phone number of someone who will always know your whereabouts

Personal History for Awards, Questionnaire or Survey
Ask for personal history as material for awards to be presented.

▸ If married, how long?

- Children's names and ages.

- Occupation.

- What college did you attend, degree earned?

- Second college, Graduate and Postgraduate degree, year earned?

- How many children, grandchildren? Expecting date?

- How far will you travel to attend the reunion?

- How many reunions have you attended?

- Did you marry your high school sweetheart?

- How close do you live to the school, military base or family homestead?

Possible Memory Book Material

- Request old school/family/military era photographs

- Who were your favorite teachers/commanders?

- What was your favorite song or musical group of our era?

- What are your hobbies?

- What was the funniest/most memorable event since we saw you last?

- Are there any anecdotes/stories from yesteryear you would like to share?

    One high school reunion committee included the question: "In high school I wanted to have a career as a _____, I ended up a _____." The more interesting answers can be included in your memory album.

    If you are incorporating personal biographies into a memory or family history book, assign someone the task of editing and organizing the responses. Leave space on the questionnaire, or on the reverse of the response sheet. Ask respondents to briefly describe what has transpired in their lives since you last met.

A 25-year reunion committee from an east coast high school compiled a list of public issue-oriented questions and published the results in their memory album. Responses were entered into a computer database. The results were categorized and shown in percentages of the total class and by male and female responses. Occupations, education levels and views on such issues as abortion, drugs and gun control were presented. It was a fascinating look on how perspectives change over time. You could even do a gag version of this, i.e., sexual mores and experience level now versus then.

> ■ **Set up a database for award winners.**
> ■ **Prepare a questionnaire or survey and**
>   **index the responses.**

Optional, however, Recommended for Fundraising

▸ Enclose a business card and check for $_____ per card to advertise in our memory album, newsletter or other handout.

▸ Ask for donations to help those who can't afford to attend the reunion?

▸ Please make a donation to the school/charity/alumni association or scholarship, even if you cannot attend the reunion.

Questions Requiring Committee Follow-up

▸ Help on the public service project, charitable donation, fundraising.

▸ Can you donate a door prize?

▸ Is there someone from our group that you know would like to attend the reunion, but cannot afford it? Assure respondents that answers will be kept confidential.

▸ Help on the reunion committee? Give suggestions for what is needed, e.g., graphics, mailing, phoning, video assistance, set up, clean up or computer assistance?

Other Requests

▸ *Whom would you most like to see at the reunion?* If you ask this question, try to use the answers constructively. In other words, during the phone drive you can say, "Dave Jones said he is hoping to see you there."

▸ *What teachers/officers would you like us to invite to the reunion?*

▸ *What were your favorite activities in high school/the service/growing up?* Code common groups – the tennis team, drama club, chess club, swim team, etc., and add this information to the lists of members and note who will be attending the reunion under the headings of these groups.

▸ *Send in a current family picture for a photo collage.*

▸ *Can you send us any memorabilia, pictures, recipes, quilt contribution or slides for display at the reunion (or use in family history documentation)?* (Slides could be used for a slide show or video.) Ask respondents to clearly identify the property if they want it returned.

Other Enclosures

▸ Response Label or Envelope. Make it as easy for alumni to respond by providing a pre-addressed return envelope or label. However, to keep postage costs down, make sure this insert does not cause the mailing to weigh more than one ounce.

▸ Hotel/restaurant brochure

▸ Discount fares and other travel information

Sample announcements and questionnaires used by two class reunion planners are shown on the following four pages. Thank you Ron Barnett and Kathryn Wentland.

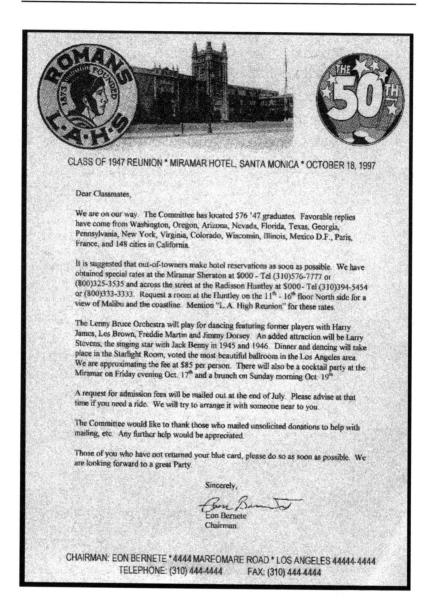

CLASS OF 1947 REUNION * MIRAMAR HOTEL, SANTA MONICA * OCTOBER 18, 1997

Dear Classmates,

We are on our way. The Committee has located 576 '47 graduates. Favorable replies have come from Washington, Oregon, Arizona, Nevada, Florida, Texas, Georgia, Pennsylvania, New York, Virginia, Colorado, Wisconsin, Illinois, Mexico D.F., Paris, France, and 148 cities in California.

It is suggested that out-of-towners make hotel reservations as soon as possible. We have obtained special rates at the Miramar Sheraton at $000 - Tel (310)576-7777 or (800)325-3535 and across the street at the Radisson Huntley at $000- Tel (310)394-5454 or (800)333-3333. Request a room at the Huntley on the 11th - 16th floor North side for a view of Malibu and the coastline. Mention "L.A. High Reunion" for these rates.

The Lenny Bruce Orchestra will play for dancing featuring former players with Harry James, Les Brown, Freddie Martin and Jimmy Dorsey. An added attraction will be Larry Stevens, the singing star with Jack Benny in 1945 and 1946. Dinner and dancing will take place in the Starlight Room, voted the most beautiful ballroom in the Los Angeles area. We are approximating the fee at $85 per person. There will also be a cocktail party at the Miramar on Friday evening Oct. 17th and a brunch on Sunday morning Oct. 19th.

A request for admission fees will be mailed out at the end of July. Please advise at that time if you need a ride. We will try to arrange it with someone near to you.

The Committee would like to thank those who mailed unsolicited donations to help with mailing, etc. Any further help would be appreciated.

Those of you who have not returned your blue card, please do so as soon as possible. We are looking forward to a great Party.

Sincerely,

Eon Bernete
Chairman

CHAIRMAN: EON BERNETE * 4444 MAREOMARE ROAD * LOS ANGELES 44444-4444
TELEPHONE: (310) 444-4444   FAX: (310) 444-4444

Dear OHS 1973 Graduate,

Once again we are enthusiastically planning our reunion. Can you believe it's been 20 years already? A fun and informal event, with a Hawaiian theme, has been planned starting with an:

ICE BREAKER

WHEN: Friday, July 9, 1993
WHERE: Poor Bill's (118 East Wisconsin Avenue, Oconomowoc)
WHAT: A casual get-together (cash bar)

DINNER/DANCE

Enjoy a memorable evening of food, drinks and dancing. Delight your palate with the taste sensation of a sumptuous Strolling buffet with a Hawaiian flair. Choose from a variety of gourmet offerings including *appetizers, hot and cold hors d'oeuvres, carved tenderloin, chicken stir fry, a fresh fruit cabaret, a gourmet vegetable ensemble* and last but not least, *coffee* and *pineapple cheesecake* for dessert!

WHEN: Saturday, July 10, 1993

  5:45 Cocktails (cash bar) and appetizers
      (beer and soda served at no extra cost)
  6:30-8:30 Strolling buffet – continuous eating and mingling
      throughout the early evening

WHERE: At the newly remodeled Dousman Community Center
  Main Street, Dousman, Wisconsin

WHAT: This will be a time to reacquaint yourselves with your former classmates. You are encouraged to bring your spouse or guest so that they, too, can be enriched by the **CLASS OF '73**

COST: $30.00 per person by May 1, 1993
  $35.00 per person after May 1, 1993
  $10.00 after 9:00 p.m. on July 10th (buffet not included)

We are putting together a memory book which will include biographical information about you and your classmates, as well as other tidbits of information. You must return the questionnaire by May 1st to be included in the book. Regardless of whether you are attending the reunion or not, we need you to return the form! This is the only way we have to keep your address current and on our mailing list. Memory books are available to those who are unable to attend for a fee of $4.00. Please indicate your choice on the enclosed response form.

DEADLINE

For reservations, remittance and questionnaire is **May 1, 1993!!!** You will be missed if you cannot attend, but please complete the form and return it ASAP.

The 15 year reunion was a lot of fun, but we're hoping to make the 20th even better! Here's hoping we hear from all of you!

  Kathy Wargersan Wentland 555-5555
  Tilie Warge Tadd 555-5555
  Steve Tittriah 555-5555

RESERVATION FORM

NAME (include maiden name): _____

CURRENT ADDRESS: _____

_____

PHONE NUMBER: (   ) _____

SPOUSE'S OR GUEST'S NAME: _____

Please list the address and phone number of someone who will always know your whereabouts. (You wouldn't believe how hard it is to track everyone down!)

_____

_____

☐ **YES!** I am coming! Here is my check for _____ person/people

☐ Sorry, I can't make it but would like to have my address updated and information about me included in the memory book.

☐ I can't make it, but would like you to send me a memory book. I have enclosed $4.00 to cover the cost of book and postage.

☐ Include my enclosed business card for listing in the business directory of the memory book at $5.00 per card.

☐ Forget about me. I'd like to be taken off the mailing list.

> Make checks payable to: **1973 Reunion Account**
>
> Return this form and remittance by May 1, 1993 to: Sathy Kentland
> 3333 Silver Codar Road
> Ocvnomowvc, WI 55555

QUESTIONNAIRE

Please answer the following questions. (Not too lengthy!)

WHAT HAVE YOU BEEN DOING FOR THE PAST 5 YEARS? (work, hobbies, clubs, etc.)

_____

_____

_____

WHAT ONE THING (advice, news, etc.) WOULD YOU LIKE TO TELL YOUR CLASSMATES AFTER 20 YEARS?

_____

_____

_____

Please fill out entire questionnaire, including back of this sheet

BRIEFLY BRAG ABOUT YOUR KIDS (list names and ages, too).

WHAT HAS BEEN THE MOST REWARDING ASPECT OF YOUR LIFE SINCE GRADUATION FROM OHS?

DURING YOUR HIGH SCHOOL YEARS, WHAT WAS YOUR FAVORITE:

Song

Musical Group

Movie

Fad

Who was your favorite teacher?

What was your most memorable event? (keep it clean!)

What was your most embarassing moment? (optional)

WE NEED YOUR HELP . . .

1. Please send a current family or self photo for a picture collage.

2. Can you loan us any of your high school memorabilia, pictures or slides for display at the reunion? If so, send and please identify and label all photos and property for return.

   YES ☐   NO ☐

3. I'd like to help out with the reunion in some way if possible. Circle the one(s) you're interested in doing:

   making name tags   decorating   registration   donating door prizes

   video/slide show   memorabilia display   anything you need me for

THE FIRST MAILING: What You'll Need

Five or six people will be all that's necessary to help to affix labels, fold, stuff, stamp and seal the envelopes. The following items should be ready for the mailing meeting:

The Announcement with Inserts
Envelopes

The mailing envelope (#10 size) should have a reunion identified return address labels affixed or printed on the upper left-hand corner of. The recipient may be more likely to open or forward a reunion notification rather than treating it as junk mail when the addressee is not easily recognizable. **Keep any mail returned for a bad address. Invalid addresses need to be logged in and followed up on, and, you can reuse the contents.**

Return Envelopes

If it'll keep the mailing under an ounce, include a pre-addressed return envelope (#9).

Address Labels

For the guest list and reply envelopes.

Postage

Self sticking, first class stamps are preferable to bulk rate. First class mail arrives quicker, is forwarded and will be returned with a corrected address, if available. The letter will appear more personal and is less likely to be thrown away. A bulk rate permit requires cash up front, tedious sorting and weighing time and is much slower to arrive. You could save on postage costs if an organization or business will let you piggy back onto one of their mailings, but considering the cost and effort, it isn't worth the postage savings.

Rubber Stamp

Have a rubber stamp made with the committee's name and return address. A thriftier way to go rather than preprinted labels.

ENTERTAINMENT

Providing entertainment at reunions is typical. Whatever entertainment is selected, book them when the reunion date is locked in. This is especially important for summer reunions because entertainers are booked months in advance. Don't leave this component to the last minute!

In selecting the entertainment, consider the desired reunion ambiance. For instance, if talking is the focus of the reunion, is it necessary to offer dancing? Do you want the entertainer to act as a Master of Ceremonies or will that job be given to an alum or family member? Here are some ideas for entertainment:

Disk Jockey (DJ)

Depending upon how much your budget allows and the involvement level desired, a DJ can often act as the "Master of Ceremonies." Is it going to be necessary to have someone "warm up" the audience? Perhaps background music is all that's wanted. The cost can range between $500 and $1,800, depending upon the number of DJs, their celebrity status and the quality of the sound equipment.

Each DJ has his or her own style and a varied collection of music. Communicate clearly what is suitable for your group. Some DJs may have large collections of current songs but few from your era. Ask to see their song list to be sure your era is well covered. The DJ's age may be a good indicator of his predominant repertoire of songs. This is an important detail which can get overlooked. Some DJs "take over" an event. Is that what you want for your reunion? **Before hiring anyone, see them perform.**

Live Band

Again, the best indicator is to watch the musicians in action. Can they can play songs from your era. In fact, ask if they have entertained at reunions before. Do they intend to play recorded music during their break time? Some reunion committees choose to bring in their own CDs for musical filler during performance breaks.

Special appearances by entertainers that would be uniquely appealing to your group could spice up the event. Use whatever contacts committee members might have.

▸ Is there an affordable musical group that was popular during your era and is still performing?

▸ How about a popular radio disk jockey that might still be around and available. Check the Internet under Reunion Entertainers or call local public relations agencies and radio stations to see which disk jockeys are available for public appearances. Radio personalities make great MCs.

▸ Engage a professional celebrity look-a-like or other person to dress up as a well-known personality from your era to talk with guests, i.e., a politician, a popular teacher or pop singers. They could present awards and keep audiences entertained.

▸ Use a mime or two. Mimes are wonderful for breaking the ice as guests wait in the registration line and wander about during the party.

Jukebox

This can be different and a lot of fun. You can rent jukeboxes stocked with music from any era you designate. A jukebox provides nonstop music and is much cheaper than live entertainment. This way, guests can select their favorite tunes during the event.

CDs/Cassettes Playing Continuous Music

This option may work for smaller, low key reunions.

For more ideas or referrals on entertainers, ask other reunion committees from your school, catering managers of various hotels or friends who have hired entertainers.

Check the Internet or the Yellow Pages under DJ, Entertainers or Orchestras and Bands. Whatever musical entertainment you select, be sure to get references. Better yet, go see them in action!

Once the entertainment is lined up, make sure they know your song preferences well before your reunion and double check the play list with them two weeks prior to your event. Remind the sound person to keep the volume **low**. A common complaint at reunions is that background music is much too loud to hold conversations comfortably in the same room. Since talking with each other is the primary purpose of reunions, loud music can ruin the entire event.

EVENTS, ACTIVITIES and GAMES

Respondents to our first edition and survey described some interesting and fun reunion activities for class reunions. More specific suggestions for family reunions are described in Chapter 9.

- ▶ At one reunion, name tags were given out randomly to arriving guests. During the evening they were told to find the person belonging to the name tag.

- ▶ At the 50-year reunion for Los Angeles High School, the reunion chair was friends with a professional singer his age. The singer wowed everyone performing tunes popular during the big band era.

- ▶ At a high school reunion in New York City, sports teams and class officers were introduced and led everyone in singing the school hymn.

- ▶ At another reunion, approximately 100 past members of a high school class choir performed an impromptu concert.

- ▶ Former football players and cheerleaders got up and led everyone in the old school cheers.

- ▶ At a 20-year reunion for San Gabriel High School in California, an alum brought their elementary school pictures from first through sixth grade. Everyone there who attended that elementary school reconnected and enjoyed a surprise mini-elementary school reunion.

For spouses and guests of alumni/military attendees, think of offering activities or displays in which everyone can participate. Hold a dance contest using the kinds of group dances that don't require partners. This is an excellent ice breaker to get the dancing started.

▶ Have someone video the guests arriving and then show it continuously during the reunion.

▶ Ask for members of various clubs, family branches or military units to meet in a designated area.

▶ Suggest that invited teachers or other special guests say a few words. (See comments of a former teacher in Chapter 1.)

Video

Many experienced videographers specialize in taping reunions. A reunion video will likely consist of a 90-minute to two hour tape of candid shots of reunion activities and interviews of guests, intertwined with era-specific background music. Perhaps they can splice old photos - then and now shots - in. The video company often requires a guarantee of sales, if enough sales are not reached at the reunion, be prepared to pay the minimum quota.

Tapes usually sell well at reunions; however, to be certain, ask people early in the mailings if they would be interested in buying one. The cost will be approximately $25 to $35 per tape. One company in Concord, California specializes in videotaping school, family and military reunions and can travel anywhere in the United States. They will not charge the committee anything. They just require your mailing list. They send out their own letter and follow up with sales. This is the preferable option since the committee has no financial responsibility. Contact: Raines Video Productions at (800) 654-8277.

If someone from your committee is knowledgeable and so inclined, he or she could make a video. Beginning with a tour of your stomping grounds, the tape could continue with interviews of former teachers and coaches. Include footage of activities and highlights of the current reunion dinner/dance. Display it at the reunion or wait and add activities from other reunion events later. Take orders at the reunion and get a duplicating service to make copies. However, consider budgeting for an outside vendor so all reunion participants can relax and enjoy the reunion.

Slide Show

Another favorite at reunions is the slide show! Hiring a professional is expensive, so perhaps you have someone on your committee who can put one together. Photograph the pictures from your school yearbook, family album or memorabilia and make them into slides. Include historical pictures and slides of the school, an old family homestead donated by your group. Juxtapose them with current shots. Use a large screen (the hotel might have one) and show it once to seated guests. Or, set up a projector and smaller screen in another area of the room. Show it continuously so groups of people can wander there and watch it anytime during the reunion.

"The video was the highlight of the evening!" according to one alumnus who attended his 30-year high school reunion in Pasadena, California. The video toured the high school grounds and former favorite hangouts. It featured interviews with former teachers and shots from their junior high and high school yearbooks.

Bring Yearbooks

Bring yearbooks or any other photo collection. Some of your old school chums might have lost their yearbooks or albums and will relish seeing them again.

PHOTOGRAPHY

A few companies specialize in reunion photography in that they provide a booklet after the reunion. So, if you'd like that idea, try to find one. In choosing a reunion photographer, do ask to view a sample of their work. It should contain the guests' family portraits, candid shots and an address directory. If two photographers are used, the time spent waiting in line to get pictures taken will go much more quickly.

Ask the photographer, family member or other volunteer to take black and white candid shots for the collage page. The photo book can be included in your ticket price or take orders at the reunion and price them separately.

One committee member who was a professional printer from a high school in Long Beach, California, produced a professional, hardbound memory book full of candid pictures taken at the reunion dinner/dance and picnic and included alumni biographies sent in during the planning of the event. This type of book can be expensive, so try to absorb some costs by selling ads.

A PICNIC AND OTHER CASUAL EVENTS

Some casual event occurring on the day of or after a formal evening event is an opportunity for entire families to participate. It also gives those who can't afford the gala event a chance to attend another reunion function. Another get together also allows people more time to reminisce or to catch up with those who were missed at an earlier occasion. The casual atmosphere might also lend itself to a more relaxed environment in which to really connect.

A picnic in a park nearby the main event would be ideal. School reunions could even have a picnic directly on the school grounds. We can't stress enough the importance of reserving a site early as picnic areas and/or baseball diamonds are often reserved two years in advance by Little Leagues and such. If outdoor activities – baseball, frisbee, soccer or whatever is planned, request that guests bring the appropriate sports equipment.

When the details are known, mention the time and directions to the location of all events in all correspondence. Repeat the particulars during the program, in handouts, on written itineraries or on a sign at check in.

MEDIA ADS
Place Ads Announcing the Reunion

Start sending reunion announcements a year before your reunion. Send notices to local newspapers and radio stations and follow up until the reunion occurs. Reunion announcements are usually free of charge because they are considered public service announcements, PSAs. Contact your local newspapers and radio stations to find out if they offer PSAs and to obtain their procedures and formats for sending them information. Provide the essential details: School name, graduation year and reunion anniversary;

date of reunion; contact person and phone number. Follow up by calling the newspaper or radio station to see when and how often the ads will appear.

Announcements Through the Internet

The Internet has become an important link in our lives for just about everything these days and announcements about reunions are no exception. Chapter 3 discusses how to find people through the Internet and some of those sites list upcoming reunions as well. While you're on-line, look for related sites to announce your upcoming reunion.

If there is someone on your committee who has access to a Webserver, see if they can design a Webpage for your event. It can be a simple page with the reunion details or more elaborate with nostalgic pictures of people and places. Professional planners will no doubt have their own Website where your guests can purchase their tickets on-line. However, if you have your own Website, this will be an easy location to communicate with and get reunion information to your guests.

BANK ACCOUNT

Upon receiving ticket payments, open a bank account. As an extra precaution, include the names of two committee persons on the account with only one signature required to sign checks. Bookkeeping responsibilities include: making copies of checks, depositing them and recording all deposits and payments. Sample accounting ledgers appear on the following two pages. The first ledger is a basic list of attendees as ticket payments are received. The ledger on the next page shows how to keep track of ticket payments and other receipts separately.

Organize the Paperwork

As papers begin accumulating, label file folders and classify absolutely everything. Folders might contain: Committee Roster, master mailing list, phone lists, locations/entertainers, contracts, personal biographies, paid reservations, bank statements, expense

Reunion Reservations

Last (Maiden) Name	Married Name	First Name	Guest Name
Adams		Mick	Jessica
Aurit	Johns	Kathy	Bob
Baker	Wilson	Beverly	Jim
Carson	Smith	Betty	
Davenport		Bob	Chris
Davidson		Alex	
Grock		Ofer	Jean
Holstein		April	Fred
Jackson	Johns	Mary	
Simonian		Steve	
Tucker		Allen	
Turner		Ted	Jane
Warner	Rich	Judy	Jeff/Tim
Wison		Bianca	Larry
TOTAL			

Dinner Tickets $50 per person
Brunch Tickets $15 per person

# of Tkts		Amt.	Balance	
Din	Brnch	Paid	Due	Comments
2	2	$130.00		
2	2	$100.00	$30.00	Pay at door
2	2	$100.00	$30.00	Pay at door
1	1	$50.00	$15.00	
2	2	$130.00		Committee
1	1	$65.00		
2		$100.00		
2		$100.00		
1		$50.00		
1	1	$65.00		
1	1	$15.00	$50.00	
2	2	$30.00	$100.00	Vegetarian
3	1	$165.00		Hotel Resrv.
1	2	$65.00	$15.00	
23	17	$1,165.00	$240.00	

receipts, questionnaires and responses, sale items, name tags, business cards, donations, reunion announcements and media ads.

For those who do not have access to a computer, keep track of all payments in some sort of ledger format.

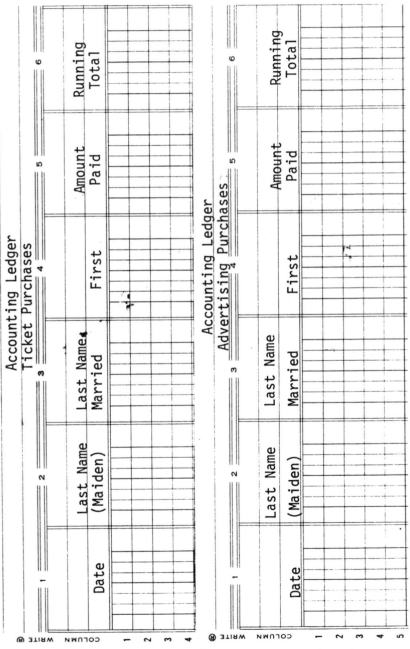

6

Create an Ambiance
Add Sizzle, Sparkle and Spirit

How do you design an exciting atmosphere? The possibilities are endless. Since attending reunions can be costly for some, the justification for going must be strong enough to overcome any kind of objection. A higher turnout derived from creating an enticing ambiance will be based on the planners' ability to communicate and sell the event. Fresh new ideas will help convince potential attendees that the reunion is an event not to be missed. By adding a unique theme or inviting special guests, for example, you just might change those nay-sayers into yes-sayers.

APPLY A THEME

Since reunions are usually tied to a nostalgic event with historical significance such as a graduation, an elder family member's birthday or military commemoration, a theme could easily be defined. Establish the reason for the reunion by applying the associated logo or idea to the invitations, decorations, souvenirs and awards: pictures of the school mascot, an ancestor's immigration ship or military vehicle are basic designs.

People are most likely to attend high school reunions in decades, the 10th being the most well attended since it is usually the first one organized after graduation. Attendance at interim 5-year reunions is typically the lowest. So if a 15, 25 or 35-year reunion is being planned, an enticing theme may be the incentive to come to the reunion.

Combine the Reunion with a Holiday

Depending upon the time of year the reunion is being held, you could accentuate a related holiday or season. Plan a costume party during October or January, a Valentine motif during February, a western focus with hayrides in April or May, a Chanukah or Christmas affair in December or an elegant dress-up affair anytime of year.

Social Action Project

A social action project would be an excellent way to give something back to the community and to add purposefulness to your reunion. A high school reunion group from Millikan High School in Long Beach, California, instituted a social action theme in all their reunions. At their 30-year reunion in 1998, two classmates spearheaded a project that involved the building of three homes for Habitat for Humanity (a privately funded non-profit organization). They also built a house for their 25th class reunion.

Another reunion committee for a school in Trois-Rivieres, Quebec, Canada commemorated their reunion by planting a tree at their school.

> *We had a tree planting ceremony at our old school during an all school reunion. It took place with the city mayor and the school principal. The oldest attending student had the honor of doing the planting.* ...Joy Malone Dudgeon

Family Project

A reunion that extends over several days will present a challenge in planning interesting activities. A theme day with related activities that any age can enjoy will work wonders. For family reunions, that could be a family tree project where everyone can participate. Suggest that everyone bring pictures and mementos. Hire a videographer or oral history expert to interview all attending family members, including children. Elder family members can tell stories and children can talk about their interests and interactions with grandparents in preparation of a family chronicle. (See Chapter 10 for a detailed discussion of genealogy and family history projects at reunions.)

HONOR SPECIAL GUESTS

The attendance of well-liked teachers or coaches may induce alumni to come to a class reunion. Invite a genealogist to speak at a family reunion. There may be a former well-liked officer that would look forward to chatting with former recruits and exchanging war stories at military reunions.

At our twenty-year reunion, we invited a well-liked football coach who retired the same year our class graduated. Well, twenty years later, looking terrific and fit as ever, Coach Nelson agreed to attend our reunion. His 84th birthday was on the same day as our reunion. During the program he came to the podium and, to everyone's delight, led us into his famous, rousing "Nelson Yell" exactly as he'd done during football games in high school. After that we sang "Happy Birthday" to him. Everyone admitted it was a highlight of the evening.

If you've hired a well-known DJ, ask if he or she has a professional photo or caricature that you could include in your reunion announcements and flyers.

Use the invitations to query alumni, family members or military buddies about possible ideas on themes. Only a few ideas may materialize this way, but they could be jewels.

MEMENTOS and SOUVENIRS

Reunions are opportunities to document personal histories and stories as a memento for those unable to come to the reunion and as a permanent record. This could be exhibited in different formats. A memory album, video, genealogy chart, oral history, cookbook, quilt and photo books are wonderful mementos and might even present the incentive to attend. (Chapter 9 discusses mementos and souvenirs specifically designed for family and military reunions.)

Memory Album

Besides current and nostalgic pictures, a memory album can be a composite of life stories, poems, letters or essays, survey results and a memorial page. This will be a cherished souvenir to hand out at the reunion. Depending on the book's cost, it can be part of the ticket price or sold separately with a little profit built in.

The simplest package is one that can be combined with a photo book prepared by the reunion photographer. Many professional reunion photographers also produce photo books. A standard book usually consists of a cover page, a committee page with a picture and comments, several pages of attendees pictures, 3 or 4 collage pages of pictures taken at the event plus a directory or roster.

A hard cover booklet is a very nice souvenir, but costly. Talk to printers and look at costs. For a little more per book, you can add pages of your own design: a memorial page, interesting anecdotes, nostalgic data like national events, fads, famous people, movies, books, songs or a sampling of consumer prices back when. Then as a way to raise additional funds, sell advertising space. Reprint business cards at a small fee per card.

▸ For class reunions, place autobiographies next to each alumnus' yearbook picture.

▸ Design a cover, a title page and an introductory page. Include a mascot, family crest or other familar logo as an identifying feature.

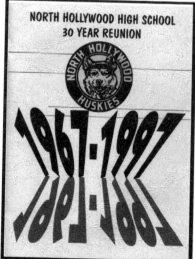

Sample title page and collage page.

▸ The title page should have the reunion date and place. The introduction page could be a statement from committee members welcoming the class to the reunion.

Include comments and feedback received after the reunion. Here are some comments received following several high school reunions:

> *. . . A wonderful evening, I wish Rocco had been there. All the girls had crushes on him.*

> *. . . I couldn't believe how much fun I could have with people I hadn't seen in 30 years.*

> *. . . I loved how everyone hugged each other, even people who really never knew each other. We made several donations to local affiliations like the elementary school, a senior citizen center, the food bank and the high school. It felt good to give back to the community in little ways.*

> *. . . It was so much fun. I hugged more people in two days than I had in 20 years! I have never felt such a sense of love and belonging as I did at that reunion.*

> *. . . What a great event. After 30 years, we had no more pretenses, we just came to be together.*

. . . It was terrific. I reconnected with many old friends I was close to growing up and had known since elementary school.

. . . The museum was a great venue. It wasn't a stuffy ballroom. I was afraid I wouldn't know anyone, but I got to see many of the guys I hung out with who were on the swim team and who I grew up with.

. . . I'm just so glad I came. I really appreciated all the efforts so many made to get to the reunion.

Comments from attendees of 50-year reunions...

. . . A reunion is when what's left of us gets together to see what's left of us.

. . . Our reunion was in October in Minnesota. The weather was perfect. The temperature on the day of the picnic was 77 ° with all the autumn leaves. We had 10 classmates who had never been to a reunion and they loved every minute. We even had four 68 year old former cheerleaders lead us in the school "locomotive" and school song.   *. . . DeeDee and Warren Jentink*

▸ Responses from the questionnaire, such as most memorable or humorous moments, popular teachers, songs or musical groups.

▸ Yearbook pictures, the homestead or other familiar site.

▸ A memorial page

▸ Survey results

▸ Business card ads, list of contributors and special acknowledgments

Once the design and content of the memory album is complete, compare prices. Choose a printer with the best package. With the availability of desk top publishing programs, the savings may be worth doing it yourself. The local high school graphics department might even be willing to help at a reasonable cost. It could be a class project. Check with the department and look at similar work they've done.

NAME TAGS

Name tags are essential at reunions. Make as many tags in advance as possible. Begin when several payments are received. Yearbook pictures should be included for class reunions. Pictures make it easier to identify people, they stimulate introductions and conversations and serve as payment confirmation.

Button Badges

These may be more expensive but are the most sturdy and make nice souvenirs. Rent or buy a button machine or look in the Yellow Pages under "Buttons." It will be cheaper if you supply the artwork yourself. The buttons should not be smaller than 3 inches. (The artwork for the 3 inch button shown below was made in Photoshop™.)

Make Your Own

Photocopy yearbook pictures on a good copier. A printer can copy or offset name tags on their superior machines. For greater visibility, enlarge the yearbook photos (this is especially helpful for 25-year reunions and up).

Sample button name tag.

Ask someone who is good at calligraphy to write the names on the tags or print them from a computer. Then apply glue stick or rubber cement and affix the pictures on the tags (you could laminate them too). Place tags in the plastic badge holders sold in most stationery or office supply stores. These holders can be pinned or clipped to clothing. Self-adhesive tags, Velcro strips, double sided tape or other adhesive will only stick to clothing for one day reunions.

Natt Collura of Vernon New York wrote us recommending that name tags at military reunions include the division logo along with the ship or unit number. Family reunion name tags can include a family crest or be color coded to each family unit for easy identification.

- **Print names on Avery Name Tag Labels™ or on self adhesive labels in your preferred colors.**

Whatever approach is used, it is recommended that name tags be prepared in advance. Bring supplies to the reunion to make name tags for last minute arrivals.

In the interest of saving space, include only the maiden surname on female alumnus' tags or both the maiden and married surnames. If both surnames are used, accentuate the name most people will remember. Prepare name tags without pictures for non-members and spouses. Use letters large enough to be seen at a distance. One rule of thumb is to increase the letter size by 5 points for each year after graduation.

TICKETS and ACKNOWLEDGMENTS

Tickets are an added cost to produce and mail, but can be a nice memento. The reception process will be much less complicated if guests arrive with tickets in hand. The registration desk workers should have a paid reservation list handy, in case someone forgets their tickets.

Create custom designed tickets or order tickets at a local print shop. Apply a logo, family emblem other identifiable picture as a background. A serrated ticket stub will be useful for door prizes and food confirmation. (See sample on following page.)

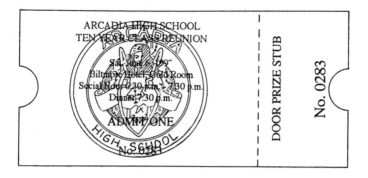

The tickets can be both a practical item and a souvenir.

A less expensive method would be to use a role of movie ticket stubs to be given to each guest in their registration packets. These are available at most party or stationery stores. The double rolls are best for selecting door prize winners.

If tickets are not sent out in advance, indicate how tickets will be handled in all reunion correspondence. For example, "Your canceled check is your receipt. Tickets will be held at the door." Many event coordinators use the registration packets as "tickets" and the name tags act as payment vouchers for the meal. The reservation or attendance list is a backup payment verification for registration table workers.

ACKNOWLEDGMENTS

Record and acknowledge payments promptly. The bulk of the ticket money will usually arrive by the deadline with the lowest ticket price, and again just before the reunion as people will wait until the last minute to pay or to decide whether to attend. Mention in your mailers how ticket payments will be handled so when alumni send in their money, they will know what to expect.

Acknowledgment Postcards

Respondents who mailed in their money need some confirmation that their check was received. A postcard acknowledgment is relatively inexpensive and easy. Purchase blank postcards and have a general receipt message printed on them. Include the date, time and place of the reunion and the number of tickets they purchased. In addition, mention how and if tickets will be involved.

Accounting Guidelines for Ticket Purchases

Indicate on your accounting ledger, those guests who have paid. If you are using index cards, highlight the paid purchasers with a noticeable mark or colorful sticker. Make copies of all checks before depositing them in the bank. This essential backup is a verification for all payments.

- **Enter all receipts for each person as payments arrive.**
- **Print labels for paid guests for acknowledgment postcards**

Write the letters AC for "Acknowledgment Postcard Sent" on the copies of deposited checks or in an accounting ledger as a verification that one was sent.

Thank you for your reunion ticket payment for ___ reservations to the millennium Notre Dame High School 30 year reunion.

Your tickets will be held at the door.

See you for the festivities beginning Friday, June 9, 2000.

The Reunion Committee

Ms. Sharon Meyer
1234 Palm Drive
Beverly Hills, CA
90210

Sample postcard acknowledgment.

Getting People There

Secrets to a Successful Turnout

The larger the attendance, the more exciting the reunion! Reunion memories are more highly cherished as the ratio of recognizable guests increase. A common goal among reunion enthusiasts is to get as many people as possible who can be found to attend the reunion. Careful investigation and perseverance will result in a high turnout. Ideas for finding people are in Chapter 3. This chapter focuses on encouraging those who have already been found to attend the reunion.

Use every means at your disposal to encourage reunion attendance – attractive mailers, personal contact through phone drives, media announcements, Internet notices and word of mouth. We also offer responses for those who, initially, might be reluctant to attend; in other words, *Don't take no for an answer.*

MAKE YOUR REUNION REALLY ENTICING

Making your reunion sound like the event not to be missed involves skillful communication. Inviting special guests and having appealing entertainment and fun activities are all strong selling points. Direct mail is the most common way to inform people about a reunion. If the notices are to produce attendance, they should be informational and graphically interesting.

MAILINGS

Encourage input by soliciting ideas on possible reunion locations or entertainment ideas. Send a questionnaire well before actual planning takes place. Good ideas will come of it and more people will feel part of the event if they had a role in planning it.

Since direct mail is the most prevalent method of informing people about the reunion, make the notices eye catching, informational and interesting. Include illustrations: a high school mascot or emblem, the family crest or military service logo. Use computer clip art. If a theme party like a "sock hop" is planned, embellish the invitations with related drawings or pictures.

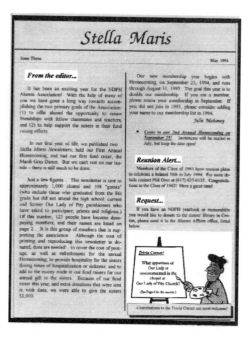

Thank you to Doris Fantini of Somerville, MA for sending in her alumni association newsletter with clever cartoons and reunion updates. The Stella Maris is the name of her former school's yearbook.

THE PHONE DRIVE

Making personal contact with as many potential attendees as possible will boost your attendance immensely. It is easy to ignore or forget about written correspondence. A phone call from a familiar person is always more effective. It lets the person know how much their presence is desired. Much of that will be missing, however, if professional reunion planners do all the solicitation work. Remember, it takes effort if you want a quality reunion.

Try to organize one meeting per month for the phone drive. Holding monthly meetings at someone's office to make calls will accomplish a great deal. Comradarie will bolster callers because people are always more focused and motivated working together on a common goal. Even if just two or three people can meet to make calls, the time will be well spent. Meeting regularly also helps to remind, nudge and focus attention on the reunion. If meeting regularly is not feasible, divide the phone lists among committee members to make calls at home.

As the committee members are making calls, remind them to ask for any information on the whereabouts of the "missing." Getting a phone number of someone who will always know how to reach them will also be helpful. Callers should note all responses from phone drives on their lists. These comments will be very useful for future phone drives. Ask callers to please be responsible for giving any "new" information (address, phone or name changes) to the person in charge of updating the main address list.

■ **Print phone lists and divide it among all volunteers.** The lists can be sequenced by area codes so people do not have to make toll calls.
■ **Write down responses and follow-up details in the comment section.**

Regular phone calls also help with some following roadblocks.

▸ **Procrastination and Indecision.** People put things off until the last possible moment. In fact, even when people live close to where the reunion is being held (since they don't need to make travel arrangements), many still will not commit to going until the day before the reunion. Repeated reminder calls will help solve this problem and perhaps lessen last minute food ordering dilemmas which inevitably occur. Valerie Anderson from Salt

Lake City, Utah lamented, "I definitely felt like I was in a catering nightmare when I heard through the grapevine that 50 more people were coming than had RSVPed."

▸ **Forgetfulness and Disorganization.** Many people misplace, lose or put aside mail that doesn't require immediate attention. Again, a personal phone call is hard to ignore and people are generally happy to be reminded.

If an office situation is not feasible, print lists by area code so volunteers can make local calls from home.

THE SECOND MAILING

As you prepare for another large mailing, make sure your address list is updated. This mailing should have more specific information on the reunion.

The Announcement

This mailing goes to the entire group again, minus those whose letters were returned. While several responses may have been generated from the first mailing, everyone should still get the second mailing.

If you are working with professional planners, be sure to insist that non-revenue generating event details are included in all announcements. They may be reluctant to advertise such events since their fees are tied only to ticket sales.

Payment Request

If you haven't already requested money for ticket purchases, do so now. To encourage early responses, set one or two deadlines with discounted fees. A sample payment schedule might look like this for a June 10th reunion date:

By April 30th . . . . $60 per person, $110 per couple
By May 31st . . . . $65 per person. $125 per couple
At the Door . . . . $70 per person

Or, with only one price break:

By May 1st . . . . $60 per person
June 1st and thereafter . . . . $70 per person

While not typical, some reunion committees offer refunds up to a certain date. If refunds are offered, stipulate that ticket payments will only be refunded until a specific date and keep a portion of the ticket price for the inconvenience.

List of Missing Persons.

■ **Identify all alumni with known addresses as "Found."**
■ **Mark as "Found" all those who responded.**
■ **Mark off deceased persons**
■ **Print list of Alumni Not Found.**

Hotel Flyer or Information on Accommodations

If the reunion is at a hotel or one is nearby, and you were able to work out a discount room rate, see if the hotel has a small flyer to include in your mailing. It should be lightweight enough to keep the mailing under one ounce. Otherwise, just include the overnight accommodation information and your group's discount room rate in the announcement.

Address Labels and Envelopes

As with the first mailing, a #10 envelope should serve as the main mailer. To avoid using envelopes, an 8½ x 11 inch newsletter or one page announcement can be folded in thirds and stapled or taped. However, this method might be bulky and awkward and not conducive for additional inserts. As for the address labels, make sure you omit those for people whose first mailer was returned.

- Print labels for all "Found" alumni.
- Print address labels of the reunion headquarters for reply cards or envelopes.

Return Envelopes or Labels

If you have room for inserts, include a reply envelope, #9 works best. Print return address labels or use the committee's return address rubber stamp.

Postage

In calculating the necessary postage, be sure to exclude the amount of returned letters from the first mailing. Purchase self-sticking stamps. This wonderful advancement has made a significant impact in the preparation of large mailings, and us reunion planners are extremely happy about it.

HOW TO ENCOURAGE RELUCTANT PEOPLE TO ATTEND

Undoubtedly, as you contact potential reunion attendees, you will discover many are reluctant to attend reunions apart from any geographical, financial or bad timing reasons. While it may seem bewildering, disinterest is one problem all reunion organizers face. Committee members work hard to make the reunion a special event so disinterest can be very disheartening. Apprehensions can range from ambivalence to reluctance at being seen. Such anxieties could stem from high school insecurities, fears that they might not be as successful or look as good as they would like or thinking no one they know will be there.

Have the main list available when calling people and offer to check on the whereabouts of those being asked about. Better yet, if numbers are available, encourage the inquirer to call. Listed below are a few replies to some common concerns. Give a copy of this chapter to volunteers to read before making their calls.

▸ *"I don't know if I'll remember anyone."* You'll see former classmates, extended family members and military buddies that you haven't seen in years. Especially interesting are those people you forgot you knew.

▸ *"No one I know will be there."* Tell committee members to ask people who they would like to see at the reunion. If the whereabouts are known, encourage the ambivalent one to contact them. If the whereabouts are not known, get any additional information on the "missing one" so the committee member can try to find him or her.

▸ *"I probably don't have anything in common with people I haven't seen in ___ years."* Fill in any number. The answer will be the same. It is amazing how much we **do** have in common with people we haven't seen in many years, since we all have had similar evolutions. Even if we've changed a lot, you will truly enjoy connecting with people who shared your formative years.

▸ *"Nothing has changed in my life. I am too embarrassed to go."* Many are disheartened if they've had little progress in their lives. Let them know that people are going to great efforts to come to the reunion and traveling long distances hoping to see you! People don't see what you have or haven't accomplished, they just see you. The ironic fact is that the naysayers are usually the ones who have the best time.

▸ *"I'm too fat. I look old. I'm divorced and unhappy. I'm unemployed, etc."* The amazing thing is we all have the same fears and shortcomings. This is why reunions are so therapeutic to our lives. People discover that no one cares how you look, your checkered past or your employment status. They just want to see you. It's confidence building knowing people just care about seeing you no matter what your perceived imperfections.

Some people didn't want to come because of the weight they had gained so we started telling people we weren't charging by the pound. Everyone found that amusing and those who had concerns came anyway.
                                                            . . . Valerie Anderson

▸ **"I hated that time of my life, why should I go to a reunion and be reminded about it?"** The reunion is an excellent opportunity to dispel old fears and haunting memories. After seeing former classmates and rivals as adults who have the same problems and experiences, former jealousies and resentments not only fade, they disappear. In fact, this may be a healing process for many.

One alumni told a reunion committee caller that she resented the way she acted toward her in high school and accused her of being snobbish and conceited. Astonished by this reaction, the committee member apologized for her actions in high school, blamed them on her immaturity and was anxious to see her again.

Letting go of old resentments and intimidations is not easy. Nevertheless, a reunion is a perfect opportunity to ally such fears and begin the healing. The happy ending to this story is that she attended the reunion and each reunion since then.

For a 50-year reunion from Gardner, Kansas, Mr. Jakobe wrote us: "What did I like most about the reunion? The fact that everyone including spouses and reluctant guests enjoyed themselves."

Reunions can often serve as motivations to improve upon one's perceived unfavorable situation. At a 50-year reunion, in Eagan, Kansas, the reunion was the incentive to stay alive:

One active committee member had, over the years, eight heart surgeries. For the two years that our committee met, she was in and out of the hospital. Doctors said they could do nothing for her. She said "I'm going to make it to the reunion." –She did–all three events. She was so happy, you'd never know she was ill. She died two days after the reunion.
                                            . . . DeeDee Jentink of Eagan, Minnesota

After thoroughly enjoying her high school reunion, an author, who originally was repulsed at the thought of attending her high school reunion, wrote a book entitled, *How To Survive Your High School Reunion . . . and Other Mid-life Crises.* She had many humorous, but poignant comments for reluctant high school reunion attendees:

> And it is predominately to this sector, haters of high school memories, that this is addressed. For I, too, grew squinty-eyed and suspicious about the emotional and behavioral backlash I'd suffer by re-exposing myself as an adult to that adolescent pecking order.
> To admit that I went, after years of oh-no-not-EVER speeches, is indeed humbling. But the next confession makes the preceding one benign. I HAD A WONDERFUL TIME. Beyond wonderful.[1]

According to an article in *Psychology Today*, a study based upon 482 surveys of reunion attendees was conducted by two psychologists on "Why People Go or Don't Go to Their High School Reunion." They highlighted an interesting observation and conclusion:

> . . . the overwhelming majority of people had a marvelous time, despite initial apprehensions. More than 90 percent of our attendees would return again. So why not take the risk? The odds of having a good time are in your favor. [2]

The study suggested that once hesitant people go to their reunions, they will have a wonderful time. They just need to give themselves the opportunity.

The article also revealed a common finding: "Reunions mean renewing friendships, reminiscing with a small group of close friends and making comparisons with others. Perhaps more

---

[1] Judy Markey, How To Survive Your High School Reunion ... and Other Mid-life Crises, Chicago: Contemporary Books, 1984, pages 3-4.

[2] Douglas H. Lamb and Glenn D. Reeder, "Reliving Golden Days," Psychology Today (June 1986): pages 22-30.

important, reunions appear to be catalysts for reflecting on our own lives and reaffirming our sense of belonging." [3]

You may have more ideas to get people to attend. Good luck, try not to get discouraged and don't give up on anyone too easily.

---

[3] Lamb and Reeder, "Reliving Golden Days," page 26.

6 Months
Before the Reunion

8

Reunion Decor

Decorations, Displays and Other Delights

As the event draws nearer, attending to details take on greater urgency. Attention to the reunion decor is as important as the entertainment, and it doesn't cost as much. Choose a decor that reflects comfort and fun.

DECORATIONS, DISPLAYS, MEMENTOS

Balloons, Balloons Everywhere

Balloons are inexpensive and are quite festive. Large individual clumps of balloons at the entryway and around the room give the impression of fun. Stephanie Gawley of Prairie High School put balloons on every chair at her high school reunion.

TABLE CENTERPIECES

Refer to your budget for the allotment for table centerpieces. Come up with design ideas that will fit. Perhaps, someone in your group is artistic and can help.

Floral Arrangements

This could be costly on a limited reunion budget. However, a small arrangement with your own trimming of balloons and colorful metallic paper, fresh flowers will be more affordable.

If your reunion is in May or June, order the flowers quite early because these months are the busiest in the floral industry with weddings and Mother's Day. In selecting a florist, look at pictures of other similar events they have handled. The hotel or restaurant sponsoring your reunion may have a florist they use.

Helium Balloons Attached to a Decorative Centerpiece

Vendors can deliver or assemble the helium balloons on the day of the reunion. Check with the location for the soonest the room will be available that day.

You could rent a helium tank and have committee members inflate the balloons on reunion day. Plan to have **at least** five or six people and several hours for blowing up balloons. Be careful not to overinflate them. You run the risk of using up the helium. This is what happened to one 20-year reunion committee.

After blowing up only 80 of 100 balloons ordered, we used up all the helium. We frantically called a committee member on her way to the reunion and asked her to bring twenty more inflated balloons. It was fortunate the party supply store was still open and all the balloons fit in her car.

. . . Sally Lawrence, Pasadena, CA

Tie centerpieces to a theme. They should be eye catching and fun.

Since set up time on the day of the event will be valuable, we recommend leaving the chore of blowing up balloons to the experts. However, whether you or a vendor needs to assemble balloons on reunion day, make sure the facility has the space and time available.

Wicker Baskets Filled with Tissue Paper in Your Preferred Colors

Anchor helium balloons to a heavy object inside the basket. Make copies of important documents related to your event: your diploma, a graduation program, passports, a family crest, pictures of commissioned posts, ships, etc. Have them laminated and attached to decorative sticks. Scatter colorful confetti (in your colors) on the table.

Potted Plants

Decorative pots filled with attractive plants could function as centerpieces, door prizes or even an auction item. The door prize winner is the one with a sticker under his or her chair.

Wine Bottle with Personalized Label

A good bottle of wine with a personalized label can serve multiple functions. Add balloons, ribbons and other accents. This unique display and/or door prize will be a hit at any reunion. A winery in California called Windsor Vineyards produces excellent bottled wines and will put any inscription you want on the labels. They have many suggestions for inscriptions if you can't think of one, but I chose one that fit our reunion theme:

Special Wines for Special Friends
North Hollywood High School
30 Year Reunion

They cannot send wine through the mail in some states. In that case, have the wines shipped to someone in your group that lives in an allowable state who will bring the wine to the reunion. Call Windsor for their list of deliverable states. Two label samples appear on the following page. They can be reached at (800) BUY-WINE or, (800) 289-9463.

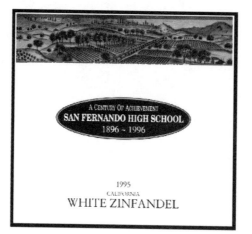

Sample wine bottle labels provided by Windsor Vineyards.

BANNERS

A canvas banner is strong enough to last for many reunions. For about $100 you'll have a permanent spirited welcome to arriving guests. Check with local sign companies, printers or the Yellow Pages under "Signs" and call for competitive bids. Paper signs are less expensive, but for long term usage, we recommend a canvas or cloth sign. It will be well worth the initial investment.

Ron Barnett, chairperson of his 50th reunion from Los Angeles High School, borrowed a 30-foot banner from his school to use at his reunion. As another display, rather than giving away prizes, he listed reunion statistics such as "who came the furthest" on a sheet of paper at each table. If you are planning a sit-down dinner, consider having a seating chart. While it involves more work, it is definitely a crowd pleaser. This way, everyone knows where everyone who showed up is sitting. A committee member from Ron Barnett's class drew a picture of their seating chart. It was blown up, mounted on a foam core and set on an easel near the check-in tables. In addition, a list of attendees with their table numbers was placed inside each registration envelope.

PICTURE BLOWUPS/POSTERS

For a nostalgic touch, copy pictures from your yearbook, have them enlarged, mounted on poster boards and placed on tables or easels. Enlarging the class group photo (sample on a following page), the family tree, passport photos, old newspaper stories, immigration papers and other related materials and photos will contribute toward the ambiance. One class reunion committee enlarged pictures of all their teachers at the reunion. Check with the facility on their rules for using nails or tacks on the walls. Easels and bulletin boards may be your best alternative.

Senior class group photo blown up for reunion.

Hang up movie posters popular during your former years. A store in Hollywood, California has a large selection of movie posters at costs ranging between $10 and $600, depending on their popularity. Call for availability and prices on the posters of your era. Located on Hollywood Boulevard, they are aptly called: Hollywood Movie Posters: (213) 463-1792.

MEMORABILIA

Nostalgia Table

A table with various nostalgic artifacts is easy to set up. For class reunions, look for varsity athlete sweaters, yearbooks, school newspapers, uniforms, regulation booklets, the graduation program, letters from classmates unable to attend, photo albums from previous reunions, books, dedications, etc.

Displaying nostalgic pictures at family reunions is especially poignant. Ask guests to write their names on the back of their pictures to insure they are returned.

Napkins, Linens, Glassware

Cocktail napkins and coasters in the appropriate colors imprinted with the school logo, family name or other identification, date of the reunion and year you're celebrating is a pleasant memento. These items can be ordered at most print shops, party supply or stationery stores.

If the facility provides table linens, select your preferred colors. If you are renting linens from an outside vendor, check your budget to see if you can afford linen napkins too. Linen napkins are more elegant, but might be budget unfriendly. Colorful paper napkins are less expensive and will serve the same purpose.

They can rent dinnerware, glassware and silverware. If that is too expensive, purchase heavy-duty plastic ware.   Otherwise, include these items in the per person food cost. The caterer should provide drinking water, pitchers, glasses and coffee cups too. Make sure coffee and tea is also included. Whoever is providing the bar service usually supplies glasses and cocktail napkins.

In Memorandum

It is always a kind tribute to remember those from your group who have died. A display of their pictures and names would be a thoughtful and respectful acknowledgment. Stephanie Gawley of

Prairie High School in Vancouver, Washington had one table set aside with pictures and flowers in memory of deceased classmates at her reunion.

Picture Collage

If you requested pictures, assemble a collage of pictures from those who responded. Display it on a poster board or have it framed. In a reunion mailing, Ms. Gawley asked alumni to answer the question, "Where are they now?" She prepared a poster board that displayed the responses.

Photographs

People often bring cameras to their reunions and never get a chance to take pictures or forget to bring one altogether. As a way to raise extra money, have the photographer or someone not associated with the reunion take group shots and offer them for sale. Or, buy disposable cameras and sell them at a mark up at the registration tables.

Joy Malone Dudgeon wished that had occurred at her all school reunion in Quebec, Canada:

> I'd have picked up several [pictures] but wasn't offered the opportunity. I took my camera to each event but couldn't bring myself to interrupt our catch up conversations and teary reminiscing to step back and say 'strike a pose!' I brought many rolls with me and shot one.

RENTALS AND INSURANCE

Dance Floor/Section Dividers

A dance floor is essential. Most facilities with banquet halls have them. If not, you should rent one. Check a few rental agencies for prices. You may incur an additional charge if an after hours pick up is necessary.

If the room doesn't provide a clear separation between the dining tables and reception area, consider renting section dividers or lattices. They will help the flow of your event and enhance the appeal of the dining area.

Audio Visual Equipment

Many restaurant/hotel facilities will rent audio visual equipment to groups holding events at their location. An outside vendor will most likely need to pick up their equipment that evening which may incur additional costs. If you do use AV equipment, verify that the location has the electrical power and accessibility, especially if your reunion is outdoors.

Insurance

If you are renting a facility that is not a hotel or restaurant, you will probably need to purchase event liability insurance. This is a good idea. It protects the committee sponsoring the reunion as well as the facility. Purchasing a one-day-event policy can be expensive. Adding a rider to a committee member's homeowner insurance policy is less costly.

REUNION ITEMS FOR SALE

Offering items to sell will help raise additional funds. Besides offering mementos and helping to balance the bank account, having a financial cushion will help to:

▸ cover miscellaneous or unforseen expenses,

▸ give a donation to charity or to your alma mater,

▸ maintain a stipend for the next reunion.

All parties benefit. The committee gets additional cash and people go home with appreciated mementos. Specialty items to order in bulk might include a video of the reunion, glassware, coffee cups, T-shirts, pens, caps and wine. Things the committee could make and sell might be family cookbooks, memory albums or a business directory. One reunion committee chair reproduced copies of her group class photo and sold them at her reunion.

If the reunion date is inscribed on the item for sale, it must be sold during the current reunion. However, if the date and place are left off, the items can be sold at subsequent reunions.

Alternatively, if inscriptions are imprinted on glassware, for instance, the item can also be an award or door prize or even a gift to an especially hardworking committee member. In fact, the entire reunion committee should get a memento of as an appreciation for all their work on the reunion.

T-shirts, Sweatshirts and Golf Shirts

T-shirts, sweatshirts and/or golf shirts are perfect as reunion souvenirs because anybody can wear them, they're affordable and profitable. T-shirts can be ordered in your preferred colors with logos, emblems, pictures or whatever else you come up with. The T-shirts in the pictures shown are from high school reunions. One is from a 25-year class reunion the other was for a class reunion celebrating turning 60.

Depending on your expected turnout, T-shirt vendors bring pre-made T-shirts to the reunion. If they sell out their supply, they can always order more.

REGISTRATION TABLE GREETERS

It is a distinct advantage to have enthusiastic volunteers greeting guests at the registration tables. Friendly greeters immediately put people at ease. It also creates an important "good first impression" especially for anyone who may be feeling a bit awkward or nervous. In fact, it probably sets the tone for the whole event.

At a 25-year reunion, the ten year old sons of two of the committee members wore their fathers' original high school varsity athletes' sweaters and greeted guests as they arrived.

These alumni had a reunion that celebrated turning 60.

Registration responsibilities include checking people in, handing out packets (and possibly souvenirs), collecting payments and directing guests to the photographer. Committee members can assume these roles, however, if they prefer not to, perhaps spouses, friends, co-workers or family members can help. Someone from the committee needs to be near the area to deal with questions or problems.

Try to enlist more people than you think is necessary to work at the registration tables. By reunion time, if it turns out fewer people are available, there should be sufficient coverage. Having extra help will allow workers to take breaks or work shorter shifts.

It will be wise to have at least two to three people handing out registration packets. At least two more people are needed at the will-call table, especially if cash is involved which takes more time. Extra assistance will reduce errors and reduce waiting time.

9

Special Tips for Family and Military Reunions

THE BRANCHES HAVE IT

Planning a family event for people that don't see each other very often is probably close to the top of the personal stress meter. Family reunions, as opposed to class reunions, can entail many different emotions that have long-lasting effects. Being related to those you're reuniting can inspire great accolades or radically alter the family dynamics.   How's that for pressure?

Military reunions don't have such tensions, but the emotional attachment can often be as strong. Typically, organizers are retired personnel who plan regular reunions. They might even belong to several squadrons or units and attend frequent reunions. Therefore, they have become quite resourceful at organizing these events.

Based on current research and input from family and military reunion planners, this chapter offers ideas and tips on some more common challenges they face.

131

FAMILY REUNIONS

Generally, family reunions take place over several days and are attended by diverse age groups. Activities, games, meals and entertainment must suit a variety of tastes and personalities. Depending on the focus of the reunion, documenting or updating the family history is likely a priority.

List your family's requirements. Make organizational decisions based on those evaluations. For example, will these be annual events or infrequent occasions? What is the objective or theme of the reunion? Is it to:

▸ bring people together for the first time,

▸ celebrate a special family occasion,

▸ learn about and document your family history,

▸ study genealogy,

▸ or, just to get to know each other better?

Whether one or more reasons apply to your situation, you'll need planning assistance and answers to some following concerns:

1. Where are most family members living?

2. Are there formidable financial constraints?

3. What are reasonable travel costs for your group?

4. How many people are needed to cover minimum costs?

5. Will you have supportive family members that can plan different portions of the event?

6. Does anyone require special consideration? disability, accessibility or other need?

7. Is there a wide diversity of ages?

Planning a family reunion also requires effective organizational skills. To review the ABCs of organization, let's *strategize, structure* and *streamline.*

WHEN AND WHERE

So, you want to plan a family reunion. As the expression goes, "Timing is Everything." Is there a unique occasion being celebrated? A special anniversary, birthday, combination of birthdays, a retirement, a return from living overseas or other milestone event? Using a theme to plan a family reunion is a practical justification that offers an incentive to attend.

An event that coincides with another important family occurrence as a wedding, confirmation, bar/bat mitzvah, christening or graduation is a convenient reason to get people together and opportune time to plan a reunion.

If the reunion does not involve a specific event, consider a time of year that allows you to plan activities both indoors and outdoors. Be prepared for inclement weather, however. If people are forced to stay inside for long periods with nothing to do but talk, you'll want to have plenty of indoor activities on hand. While reunions are meant for gathering and talking, long-term communal confinement could be counterproductive.

Four days to a week is a suitable time frame if this is an infrequent or first time gathering of your family clan. However, an annual park or backyard bar-b-que can be just as memorable.

Location

In choosing a location, consider a spot where the bulk of family members live or one that might have special significance to your family. Characteristic sites like your hometown, where a contingent of your ancestors lived, or perhaps an entry port where your predecessors immigrated.

> *We held our Italian family reunion in New York near where our ancestors arrived on the boat and close to the stoop of the building where our family lived for many years. This location presented many fond memories and wonderful stories that they have passed down in our family.* . . . *Patricia Parziale Papanek Los Angeles, California*

If family members are spread all over the country, you may want to select an affordable retreat to enable guests to focus their financial resources on travel. If it's feasible, visit the location, or at a minimum, get a recommendation from someone you know who has stayed there.

Chapter 2 had ideas on reunion locations. Choose one that can easily adapt to groups and offers enough space where everyone is not forced to be together all the time. Small meeting areas for those wanting quiet moments will be sufficient. Having a supermarket nearby will also be helpful, along with interesting site-seeing locales for free time excursions.

The retreat should have 911 services, a nearby emergency room, name and number of a dentist available nights and weekends, hospital equipment supply where to rent a wheelchair or crutches if necessary, and the name, address and phone number of the nearest 24-hour pharmacy.

A site that caters to family reunions will have an event coordinator to help with planning events, games and activities. Check for minimum reservation/room requirements.

ETHNIC REUNIONS
Celebrate Your Family Culture

Have you ever considered holding or attending an ethnic reunion? One way to acknowledge and appreciate your family history is to celebrate your family culture. Many family groups reunite to celebrate their heritage with folk dancing, ethnic foods, art, exhibits, music and sports traditions and customs. Some also hold discussions on their cultural history, foods, genealogy and language.

Ethnic reunions occur in the United States and overseas in different locations every year. One unique American landmark is Ellis Island, the major port of entry for 17 million immigrants between 1892 and 1954. A major part of America's history, this 27-acre island has a main building with over 4,000 exhibits and artifacts and a baggage room with original trunks and suitcases. The Great Hall tells the story of where 90 different nationalities waited for inspectors to review their entry documents and be examined by doctors. An oral history project sponsored by the United States Department of the Interior is in the works. They are soliciting the vocal retelling of experiences of immigrants who were processed through Ellis Island during those years.

Many families meet relatives at European cultural reunions that they never knew existed. Many such reunions take place every year throughout the United States. Finnfest reunions (celebrating the Finnish lineage) have occurred annually since 1983. Finns and Finnish Americans celebrate their heritage with music, folk dancing, entertainment, foods, gifts and memorabilia. Their hope is to encourage descendants to recognize, appreciate and continue their family tradition. Contact: FinnFest USA, 636 16th St, SE,Owatonna MN 55060-41200.

Greek, German, Italian, Scottish and Irish Fests (Irish Fest, 515 No. Glenview Ave, Milwaukee, WI 53213; 1-414-476-3378) also regularly occur. They also honor their unique traditions and customs by bringing people of similar cultures together, providing forums for genealogy research and raising money to maintain their rich heritage for future generations. The Upstate New York Italian Cultural Center and Museum, for example, grew out of a desire to tell the story of the Italian immigrant. This nonprofit organization sponsored by the American Italian Heritage Association houses memorabilia, artifacts and old photos for the U.S. Italian American community. Contact: Box 419, Morrisville, NY 13408.

The African American community is probably the oldest and largest ethnic group that holds regular organized family reunions. The African American Family Reunion Conferences celebrate principles, traditions and family unity in their regular three-day conferences. They feature workshops, speakers and resources in family reunion planning. This helps strengthen family bonds and community ties.

REUNION ANNOUNCEMENTS
Include an itinerary and description of the planned activities in all mailings. This will help generate interest and initiate responses. Besides talking about the reunion event, make the mailings newsy and interesting. Include a questionnaire, travel news and any marriage, birth and death announcements. Add prior reunion photos, biographical sketches of live or deceased relatives, puzzles, clip art, jokes, poems, children's art, stories and family trivia. Besides requesting an event payment, you might ask for donations to family members in financial need.

REGISTRATION

As discussed earlier, the initial reception sets the tone for the entire reunion. Greet arrivals with signs or banners. Whatever methods are used, make the initial greeting a welcomed and positive experience. Highlight the reason for reuniting on all registration handouts. Whether it's an anniversary, a birthday or just getting together, something that reminds guests why they're there. Recommend that everyone wear their name tags, including greeters, all the time.

Set up a bulletin board in a central location with announcements of each day's activities and suggested times so everyone can plan their schedules accordingly. This could be the focal point of the reunion. Include a memorabilia table here with displays, artifacts and pictures.

Start with an ice breaker. If family members brought their home videos and pictures, this might be a good opportunity for everyone to get to know each other better.

PLANNING ACTIVITIES

The main purpose of prearranged games and activities at family reunions is to provide a setting for people to talk. For multiple-day reunions, it will be a challenge to plan activities that keep people interested and busy.

Sketch out several meals together such as breakfast and dinner and allow people to be on their own for lunch. Don't have every day filled with organized activities; **people need to have time to enjoy some normal things they do while on vacation.**

Activities That Involve Children

Don't assume that children will develop their own games and activities during the reunion. Plan a few activities to allow family members of all ages to be together and some designed for children and adults to enjoy separately. You will stimulate common interests and build fond memories if children and teenagers can connect with each other on their own level.

Outdoor Activities

Ask everyone to bring their own sports equipment even if they are holding the reunion at a lodge or hotel that has these items.

Depending on the location, ask guests to bring appropriate equipment. Tennis, basketball, bicycling, soccer, volleyball, badminton, football, bociball, golf, frisbee, croquet or baseball gear are some ideas.

Of course, children can bring their own skateboards, roller blades, ice skates, fishing accessories and other sports equipment. Depending on the site's options, team sports might include basketball, baseball or soccer. Select a location with a swimming pool or is near a lake or river. The kids love to swim and everyone can enjoy the related activities.

Depending upon the time of year, activities can involve both children and adults. Scavenger or treasure hunts, croquet, golf, horseback riding, skiing, ping pong, archery and shopping are a few activities everyone can enjoy. Egg or water balloon tosses, sack and relay races, softball, volleyball and badminton are appropriate for all ages, even if some participants are just spectators.

Tip: A suggestion for all age groups. Here's a race that doesn't force people to compete against each other and involves several skill levels. Select a fixed route upon which different modes of transportation can coexist like walkers, runners, bicyclists and parents pushing baby strollers. Each group starts 10 minutes apart. Each person estimates their individual completion time. The winner is the person or team that comes the closest to predicting their own course completion time for whichever mode they choose.

Hiking, biking and walking strolls are ideal for those who enjoy nature. The entire family can participate in these activities that are designed for holding conversations. Ranger or self led tours, site-seeing tours, campfires and picnicking are also excellent opportunities to get to know each other.

Museums, attractions, parks, monuments, family homesteads and former schools and other off-site tours will complement the reunion itinerary. An event coordinator at locations that encourage reunions can offer a bevy of suggestions. If the site is not in your immediate vicinity, check with the Convention and Visitors Bureaus (CVBs). They offer free materials and information on places to hold reunions. Besides area accommodations, they provide details on transportation, attractions, events, entertainment and ancillary services such as florists, caterers and off-site tours. Many are membership organizations, however, and must represent the providers equally.

Indoor Activities

Ask family members to bring cards, bingo board games, checkers, dominoes, puzzles and art projects. Musical instruments as guitars, banjos, violins, flutes, clarinets and harmonicas travel easily. The talented musicians in your group can play while others can join by singing and dancing. Bring some instruments that anyone could play: tambourines, kazoos, bamboo sticks, bongo drums, bells and triangles.

Games and Contests

Think of games and contests that will entertain and provide information. These two games will encourage learning about the family.

▸ Ask people to send in family trivia questions or baby pictures before the reunion. One evening, play charades by forming family teams. Each team tries to answer family trivia or guess the identity of the baby pictures. Questions could be important dates, milestone events, occupations or the ownership of interesting life stories.

▸ Ask everyone to anonymously write down 6-10 interesting attributes about themselves, their likes and dislikes on a sheet of paper. Put the papers in a bowl and let each person pick one. The winner is the one who guesses the correct family member using the fewest clues.

Evening Activities

Ask people to bring home movies or videos and spend an evening sharing your photos, slides and albums. What other audience is there that will *truly* enjoy watching these home creations?

Plan a talent night where everyone can share their artistic forte. This could involve playing musical instruments, performing skits, singing and dancing. Hire a band or DJ for one night and when everyone can dress up and dance. This might be an opportunity to let the young ones have a separate evening to themselves with a pizza party and their favorite music on CDs.

Activities and tours needn't be structured every minute. Allow free time for families to plan their own activities and side trips.

Bring videos and shoot lots of film. If you hire a professional videographer, you won't have to risk a family member missing something. A more professional product will result. A professional will use quality equipment and apply editing, music and computer graphics such as adding still pictures and segments of older family films. A lower price per video can be negotiated if you provide a minimum guarantee of sales.

Ask a family member or hire a professional photographer. With a wide-angle lens, take several group pictures. Even if a professional is brought in for one day, it will be a wonderful pictorial documentation of your reunion. Prearrange a time so everyone knows when photo sessions will take place and can plan their schedules accordingly. With groups of 50 or more, you should allow 45 minutes to an hour for the set up and shoot.

Ticket Price

After all activities are planned and expenses are factored in, determine a ticket price. Mention everything that goes into the ticket price in your mailings. Remember, it's not a good idea to barrage guests with pleas for help in defraying costs or unanticipated shortfalls at the reunion. Remember, if you budget, you will balance.

SOUVENIRS, AWARDS and PRIZES
Name Tags

Name tags are important at any reunion. For a multiple-day reunion, they should be sturdy enough to be reattached each day. Self-adhesive tags are good only once. Buttons or cloth name tags work the best.

T-shirts/Caps/Sweatshirts

T-shirts are the most common family reunion souvenirs. They are inexpensive and can be worn by everyone. Add your family crest, pictures or a family tree with the names of everyone who attended the reunion. People order and pay for them ahead of time so the shirts can be worn at the reunion. To help identify family lineages, a similar color can represent each family branch. Hats, caps and sweatshirts are popular souvenirs too.

Family Cookbook

A family cookbook is not only a memorable souvenir, it is a lifelong keepsake that won't go out of date or lose relevance. It usually represents a loving tribute to the family and can serve as a historical document for future generations.

Cookbooks are easy to put together. Simply collect recipes and retype them in a consistent format. A printer or copy shop can assemble the books. A combed or spiral binding is recommended since they wear better than the glued or hole-punched versions. The cover can display a picture from a prior reunion, a family member who is being honored or other historical snapshot. To add distinctiveness, place the person's picture next to their recipe.

If your budget allows, have cookbooks professionally assembled. Many companies specifically produce family cookbooks. They provide how-to instructions and offer pre-designed covers that they can customize to your liking.

Family Quilts

Family quilts are some unique renditions of a family history. They are invaluable heirlooms that can be created and assembled at reunions and passed down through generations. Quilts usually represent the combined endeavors of many branches of the family and preserve events, experiences and people. They can be created as one group project, or if enough squares are supplied, made in multiples so every family has one.

A reunion is an opportunity to bring patches or squares that reflect each family's personal traditions. Squares can be embroidered, drawn, cross-stitched or sewn. Pictures can be scanned into computers and imprinted directly onto cloth. One California family began a quilt as a class project in a college course. It evolved into an extraordinary keepsake that reflected many parts of their family history. Squares were comprised of remaining patches of a baby's blanket, one of grandmas' embroidered tablecloths, an aunt's dress, sports emblems and piece of a cousin's wedding ring pillow.

Quilts can be auctioned at the reunion as a fundraiser or brought to each reunion as an heirloom display. A family in California received enough squares to make six quilts in honor of their first family reunion. Each quilt had an envelope in the back with the names of the committee and the significance of each patch. It was so popular that in order for each family to have it immortalized, a picture of the quilt was converted onto stationery, puzzles, posters and postcards which they sold at the reunion.

Other Mementos

Additional mementos as personalized wine bottles, pens, wine glasses, cups, key rings and other family keepsakes and souvenirs can be used for awards or as fundraising items.

Family members could donate handcrafted items for door prizes and awards. Request donations in all mailings. Once they are in hand, credit the donors. Such items could include grandma's crocheted tablecloth, quilt or bedspread or Aunt Ellen's paintings or handmade figurine.

Glassware, cups, bumper stickers, tote bags, coasters, paperweights and pennants are all popular family reunion keepsakes and can be ordered in assorted amounts. The larger the order, the lower the per unit cost. Raise money by adding a mark up factor.

Another activity that can also yield a memorable souvenir is to offer hand drawn portraits. It is not that expensive and will be a fun exercise. Hire an artist to draw charactertures of each family group.

Each person was drawn performing their favorite activity.

Award Categories

Samples of family reunion awards appear below.

▸ Oldest and youngest family member at the reunion

▸ Oldest and most recent married couple

▸ Newest parent/grandparent

▸ Youngest grandparent

▸ Most children/grandchildren/great grandchildren

▸ Largest family unit present

▸ Family that has attended the most reunions

▸ Two family members that most look alike

▸ Oldest to retire/oldest still working

▸ Most descendants

Prizes

An advantage of door prize and award donations is that they don't come out of the reunion budget. They might even have greater sentimental value. T-shirts, history books or the family cookbook can also be used for awards.

Consider prizes that coincide with the award that is being presented:

▸ Oldest and youngest family members at the reunion: *a frame later to be filled with a picture taken of the two winners at the reunion*

▸ Newest married couple: *the family cookbook*

▸ Newest parent/grandparent: *frame with a photo of both winners*

▸ Most Children: *free babysitting at reunion by family members*

▸ Largest family unit present: *free airline tickets* (hopefully someone in the family has earned and will donate free flight mileage).

▸ A family member that has attended the most reunions: *complementary tickets to the next reunion*

▸ Youngest grandparent: *attractive upcoming calendar highlighting the birthdays of all the grandchildren and an array of birthday cards with stamped envelopes*

▸ Youngest to retire: *personalized copy of* The Reunion Planner *for the person with the most time to plan the next reunion.* (See last page.)

Other Displays

Besides quilts, hand made auction items, photo albums, a family tree, cookbook, heirlooms and other memorabilia, a photo board of pictures of unidentified family members may provide the missing pieces to many unsolved puzzles. Hopefully, family members will recognize more faces.

FUNDRAISING IDEAS

There are many ways to cover reunion expenses, pay for scholarships or supplement a family member's expenses.

▸ Add a small amount to the registration fee. This is the simplest method of raising extra cash. Everyone should understand that the ticket fee covers expenses. A slight mark up reduces the need to rely on reunion merchandise sales. As an inducement for raffle sales, mention that prizes will be paid for with half the receipts. The balance collected can go toward reunion expenses.

▸ Besides selling specially ordered items, handmade donations as quilts, paintings, tablecloths, pillows or other handicrafts can be auctioned to the highest bidder. Encourage donations even from those who can't attend the reunion. If the object doesn't sell beforehand, hold a silent or live auction at the reunion. Homemade baked goods can be sold at the reunion.

▸ Some inexpensive prizes could be purchased and later personalized with family pictures as Christmas ornaments, mouse pads, glassware, coffee mugs and glassware. (Many large shopping centers and retail outlets have vendors that sell these items for less than $10 each.) There are many mail order businesses that manufacture these items at a lower cost if you order in quantities.

Order these items well before your reunion, as delivery time can take as much as 8 - 10 weeks. See if the company will send product samples so you can check them out.

▸ Sell calendars with family pictures. This is inexpensive and can be prepared before the reunion. Family members can send in photos. Combine several photographs in a collage format or use individual family pictures. (Many large copying centers will scan any picture you bring in, enlarge it and affix it in their predesigned forms.)

▸ Sell group photos taken at the reunion. Collect money, including postage costs, and send out later.

▸ Maintain a coin jar and ask guests to donate pennies and spare change and/or offer candy or other munchies less than $1 and sell at double the original cost.

▸ If your reunion and the attendees are mostly local, purchase gift certificates from your favorite hair salons, movie theaters, restaurants and speciality shops. They may even donate or offer a reduced price for your group. Offer these as auction items in early mailers and have them available at the reunion for continued bidding. Announce the winners at an evening event.

▸ Offer inducements for people to send in their ticket payments early. Provide gifts to the first ten registrants.

MILITARY REUNIONS

From all across the land they come, with just one thought in mind
To share again the memories of the days they left behind.
'Tis fifty years ago or more they stood on foreign soil
And said goodbye to friends they'd known, in blood and sweat and toil.
They are fathers, husbands, friends of many different kinds
But just for now they're veterans of another war and time.
Theirs is friendship forged in danger, and tempered under fire.

They bow their heads in tribute to those not here today
Those men who once they knew as friends, who fell along the way.

*Their ranks are growing thinner now, the passing years will tell
But they are soldiers, everyone, who served their country well.
And so they meet, embrace and talk, and remember days of your
For there is just a deep desire, to see their friends once more.
This may be their last reunion, for some it is the last goodbye
'Till they meet again in Heaven, at the great reunion in the sky.*
....***Author Unknown, Contributed by Joe Quade, 17th Airborne Division as it appeared in Reunions Magazine, August 1995.***

Soldiers share a special bond. To many of those who served in the military, a common thread is that the friendships forged and the time involved was the strongest and most influential of their lives. They formed bonds under unusual conditions and the camaraderie lasts a life time.

An anonymous memoir that appeared in *Reunions Magazine* in Winter 1997 identified the essence of military reunions.

Many of our experiences and thoughts cannot be easily shared with people we love and live with and in fact, friends and family may no longer want to hear war stories, not realizing the subtle yet profound importance they may represent.

A reunion offers many a chance to remember, fill in the blanks, rediscover long-lost friends, compare experiences, spend time with someone you had previously overlooked and be with those who understand and finally put into proper perspective that most profound part of our lives.

*. . . Anonymous
contributed by James Bethell
845th Spearheaders Association*

What's Unique About Military Reunions?

According to *Reunions Magazine*, World War II Veterans hold most military reunions, and because they usually don't involve children, their entertainment needs are different from family and class reunions.

Enrique Tabyanan of the 70th Air Refueling Association helps organize his reunions every odd year while a sister squadron holds reunions every even year. Their squadron was stationed in Jacksonville, Arizona. Like many military reunions, they hold them at or near their military base. Activities include sitting around catching up on the news of families and talking about old times. They average 210 - 235 attendance at each reunion.

The 70th Association was mostly flight crew members who spent more time together than with their families at the height of the Cold War. Consequently, their wives formed bonds of their own which make their reunions more like family gatherings.

They formed an association membership by charging dues which help to support their reunion efforts. One of their Air Force pilots started an address book in 1961. He went to work for Delta Airlines in 1966 and wherever he went he would call someone he knew, pass the news and ask for new addresses to add to the book. After 20 years, he had amassed a database of 925 names with approximately 350 members.

They typically have a welcome reception Thursday evening, a picnic Friday, a banquet Saturday night and a farewell breakfast Sunday. Upon sign-in everyone receives a squadron coffee mug, a cap and a T-shirt.

> *We just sit around and catch up on the news of family and friends, tell war stories (funny experiences we had as young flyers) which we never tire of hearing and sing the praises of comrades gone.*

Many Veterans want to preserve and support patriotic affiliations by organizing daytime tours of local historical sites and national monuments. Valley Forge in Philadelphia, Kennedy Space Center in Florida and Langley AFB, Williamsburg or the War Memorial Museum in Virginia are a few examples.

Let's not forget the women who served in the military. While smaller in numbers, women also formed strong attachments with those who shared wartime experiences. Many are bonded not necessarily by having served together, but because they trained in the same divisions. "Preserve the rich history of all air evacuation squadrons" is what the World War II Flight Nurses Association tries to accomplish. They want flight nurses who served in Korea, Vietnam or Desert Storm to join their association to maintain their unique heritage. They met in San Diego in 1994 and Philadelphia in 1995.

Battleship or Battleground Reunions

"Reuniting with a place is for some Veterans the most healing aspect of their journey," says C. Ryback Burns. He suggests planning a military reunion on the ship or battleground that made an impact on their lives. Battleship Massachusetts, for example, offers assistance in planning reunions on their ship in Battleship Cove in Fall River, Maine. They can be reached at (800) 533-3194.

Overseas reunions and tours are another way to reunite Veterans on common ground. Joe Quade, a contributor to *Reunions Magazine*, recommends getting a travel agent who is knowledgeable about military history and suggests visiting a training area and battle locations. He also recommends that you "Plan excursions near shopping locations so the whole family can enjoy the trip." Battlefield Tours, USA offers tours of European battlegrounds and are accompanied by a WWII historian. Call them at (800) 635-5018. Valor Tours specializes in Pacific and European tour reunion cruises. They can be reached at (415) 332-7850.

Organization Recommendations

Thomas Novic of the 32nd Division Veteran Association, recommends setting up a military database with categories that include name, address, phone, nickname, military unit, assignments, a yearbook buddy page with space for 6-12 names, room for up to four tours, military division, donation to drawing or raffle, banquet table number, meal preference and miscellaneous.

Mementos

Special mementos might include a collection of writings, poems, letters and stories of wartime experiences. Consolidate them all into a booklet. Add period-related photographs and write tributes to those who have died. Related military books, monogrammed caps, T-shirts, paintings and nostalgic photographs are also popular and reliable fundraising items.

Get the Word Out

Contact national veterans' organizations that publish periodic magazines. They devote sections to upcoming military reunions. The American Legion, VFW, Forty and Eight Chateaus, Veterans

Clubs, unit newspapers, local papers, membership rosters and Veterans Magazines (the Internet or libraries have lists of organizations and addresses) are just a few. National Reunion Registry and Press Services will send announcements to 2,000 newspapers and magazines at a fee per mailer. They can be contacted at (210) 438-4177. Each issue of *Reunions Magazine* lists military reunion notices in their *Reunion Reveille*.

Visit Internet Websites that connect to various military organizations that announce reunions. (See Military Search Sites in Chapter 3.)

10

Genealogy Charts and Family Histories
LEAVE IT TO THE CHILDREN

For those who create and update family histories and charts, interviewing family members at reunions is an excellent place to accumulate information. Such personal recollections will provide a wealth of data you won't find in public records or general history books. There is much to assimilate and many resources that provide research and assistance in creating genealogy charts and developing a family tree. The lesson of this chapter is on how reunions can ease that process. We also offer direction on how to start researching your roots.

GENEALOGY RESEARCH

The Church of Jesus Christ of Latter-day Saints (LDS), is an excellent resource for searching family histories. The Family History Library (FHL) in Salt Lake City, Utah houses the largest collection of genealogical material in the world. The society is dedicated to acquiring and preserving copies of the records of humankind. So that families may continue to discover their ancestors, they send specialist teams around the world to find and copy existing records. Microfilm preserves the land grants, deeds, parishes, wills, marriage certificates, cemetery and other public records that help to document people's lives.

Since 1964, Family History Centers (FHC) have been set up at locations in every State of the Union and more than 55 countries around the world. The Family History Library and their resources and materials are all available to the public free of charge except a small cost for photocopying and computer printouts. The Family History Library has more than 2,150 microfilms of US passport records, for example, from the National Archives and Department of State. The first passport was issued in 1796, but US citizens generally traveled abroad without passports until World War I. US Passport information contains applicant name, family status, birth date and place, residence, naturalization (if born outside the US) and other biographical information. To find a Family History Center near you call, 1(800) 346-6044.

They designed their FamilySearch ™ software and collection of databases on CD-ROM to simplify your research. The program works on personal computers and has files drawn from the Church's temple and family history files including:

Ancestral File ™ (AF).

Containing genealogies contributed by members of the Church since 1979. Also, find the name of the person who contributed the ancestral information.

International Genealogical Index™ (IGI).

This has information about deceased persons for whom they have performed temple ordinances and lists birth, christening or marriage dates. With more than 200 million names, you can look for a name in a single alphabetical list of persons for all major regions of the world and search the files' parent index which is helpful for finding possible family groups.

U.S. Social Security Death Index

Persons whose deaths were reported to the Social Security office (about 40 million names) between about 1962 and 1988 covering records extending from around 1937 to 1990.

The Military Index

This index lists individuals in the U.S. military service who died in Korea or Southeast Asia from 1950 - 1975. The information includes dates of birth and death, town and state at time of enlistment, the country where the individual died and some details of rank and service.

Family History Library Catalog ™.

A listing of the library's holdings and microfilm call numbers.

Personal Ancestral File ™ (PAF).

Purchase this software to set up your own family search. It is available for $15.00 including shipping charges by calling 1(800) 537-5971. This software has established a standard (called GEnealogical Data COMmunication, or GEDCOM) for the exchange of genealogical information. Now, the CD-ROM and microfiche versions provide off-site access to the indexes and catalogue at the Family History Centers. Visit or call an FHC for more information on the program and its value.

If you have information on a family history they do not have, and lend it to them to be microfilmed, they will give you a free copy of the microfilm. If you contribute a family history, rest assured this is the one place where it will be guaranteed to be around for generations to come.

Independent genealogy enterprises provide support to those who may wish to use the FHL such as Everton Publishers 1(800) 443-6325 and Heritage Quest 1(800) 760-2455. They are both in Utah and sell genealogy related products. Everton Publishers sells two copies of a 17" x 22" seven generation pedigree chart for only $2.95 including shipping. Call for free catalogues.

They also offer training and commissioned research for clients. They each run genealogical societies for sharing and distributing relevant information among their clients. Although they all have access to electronic mail services, neither these nor the FHL offer consultation services over the Internet yet. However, their respective Websites are ***www.everton.com*** and ***www.heritagequest.com.*** There is a membership fee to use their databases or accessing public records like the Social Security Death Index is free.

For a simple pedigree chart, the 8½" x 11" Ancestor and Genealogical Charts are available from 20th Century Plastics, (800)767-0778, in Brea, California (pages 155 and 156).

Broderbund Corporation has the Family Tree Maker software that explains how to preserve and organize your family history. Start by entering a few names and facts about your family. Then, click the mouse to view and print family trees, birthday calendars and mailing labels. You can enter up to two million relatives and organize dozens of additional facts about each person such as: recorded education hobbies, medical history and more. Also, include photos in each person's Scrapbook and write stories in the 15 pages of freeform notes per person.

This software reads your PAF files directly and prints standard LDS reports. Also, import and export GEDCOM files, make family trees, kinship reports and calculate how people are related. Furthermore, you can create photo albums and family books with layouts, family group sheets and individual fact sheets giving details on a person or family.

Professional genealogical societies will help find and research your family records and history. For families that want to begin or continue recording their family history, a reunion is the opportune place. Invite a speaker or researcher from a local genealogy society. They can help you to get started collecting and documenting your genealogy and family history.

Ask family members to bring copies of any historical documents such as wills, birth and death certificates, naturalization papers, marriage certificates, diplomas, military or church records, personal writings or other written accounts of your family's background to the reunion. Then write down, copy, record and videotape your family's memories and papers.

A magazine for families researching their roots began in 1996 and has six issues per year. Based in Ontario, Canada, they and can be reached at (416) 696-5488 or through their E-mail address:

magazine@familychronicle.com. They have interesting genealogy related articles and stories on many cultures, their roots, resources, software and suggested readings. They list preferred genealogy Websites that spotlight tools, surname data and interesting family histories: ***www.familychronicle.com.***

If you interviewing family members for your own family history, be sure to note who supplied the information as you may need to verify it later.

FAMILY HISTORY BOOK

A good method for documenting your background is with a family history book. This will be a treasured keepsake and will pay for itself if you price the books a few dollars over production costs.

The Parziale family put together a wonderful pictorial family history book. Before the reunion, family members were asked to send in pictures and written remembrances. Using her computer, Barbara Shapley scanned in and returned the pictures.

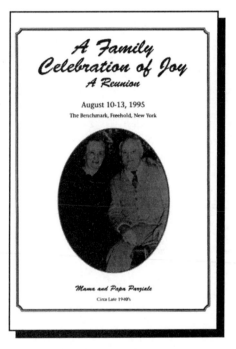

A Family Celebration of Joy
A Reunion

August 10-13, 1995
The Benchmark, Freehold, New York

Mama and Papa Parziale
Circa Late 1940's

Then, with photos, stories and family recollections, she recreated her family's immigration from Italy to the United States in the early 1900s. She wrote beautiful poetry in relating her family's entry and life in America. Her story began with the following tribute to her grandfather.

This is grandpa.
I never knew him tall and straight.
Red hair split in curly lumps

I recall
That he had no hair at all
He was grey and old.
A bald and somber man
His barber chair imprinted
—timeless—
Countless haircuts, shaves.

Razor sharp, black leather strap.
Mug of lather, short and bristly
brush
Slathered on Italian Chins of
stubble.

A Victrola sang in Neapolitan.
I thought, "Could he be the
Barber of Seville?"

What went through his mind
As he stood and posed?
Straight and tall
Slender tilt of arrogant cigar.

What I would give to meet him.
To ask the Who? and What? and
How?

Of life.

Captured only in this photo now.

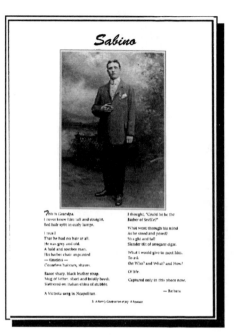

                                                        —Barbara

A family history book can be created on your own computer using any desktop publishing software or even a word processing package. Depending on the quantity you want to print, the cost of producing such a book can be very reasonable. If some family members are really ambitious, this could be an ongoing project that gets updated periodically and for each successive reunion (with photos from previous reunions). Go back further in time as more information is revealed.

The book can include pictures of homes and places where family members grew up along with other memorable sites. Copy or scan in family documents such as passports and entry visas.

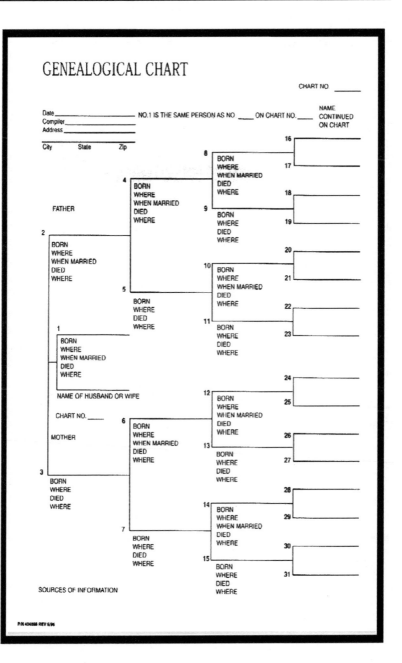

GENEALOGICAL CHART

CHART NO. _____

Date _____ NO.1 IS THE SAME PERSON AS NO ____ ON CHART NO. ____

NAME
CONTINUED
ON CHART

Compiler _____

Address _____

City   State   Zip

16 _____

8

BORN

WHERE

WHEN MARRIED   17 _____

DIED

4   WHERE   18 _____

BORN

WHERE

WHEN MARRIED

FATHER   DIED   **9**

WHERE   BORN

WHERE   19 _____

2   DIED

WHERE

BORN

WHERE   20 _____

WHEN MARRIED

DIED   **10**

WHERE   BORN

WHERE   21 _____

5   WHEN MARRIED

DIED

BORN   WHERE   22 _____

WHERE

DIED   **11**

1   WHERE   BORN

WHERE   23 _____

BORN   DIED

WHERE   WHERE

WHEN MARRIED

DIED

WHERE   24 _____

NAME OF HUSBAND OR WIFE   **12**

BORN   25 _____

WHERE

CHART NO. _____   WHEN MARRIED

6   DIED

BORN   WHERE   26 _____

MOTHER   WHERE

WHEN MARRIED   **13**

DIED   BORN

WHERE   WHERE   27 _____

3   DIED

WHERE

BORN

WHERE   28 _____

DIED

WHERE   **14**

BORN   29 _____

WHERE

7   WHEN MARRIED

DIED

BORN   WHERE   30 _____

WHERE

DIED   **15**

WHERE   BORN

WHERE   31 _____

SOURCES OF INFORMATION   DIED

WHERE

P/N 404388 REV 6/96

ANCESTOR CHART

SURNAME _____

HUSBAND _____ THE SAME PERSON AS NO. _____ ON CHART _____
BORN
WHERE
WHEN MARRIED _____ WHERE _____
DIED
WHERE
HUSBAND'S FATHER _____ CHART NO. _____ MOTHER _____ CHART NO _____
HUSBAND'S OTHER WIVES

WIFE Maiden Name _____ THE SAME PERSON AS NO. _____ ON CHART _____
BORN
WHERE
DIED
WHERE
WIFE'S FATHER _____ CHART NO. _____ MOTHER _____ CHART NO. _____
WIFE'S OTHER HUSBANDS

Child	Sex	CHILDREN of this marriage	BORN Date	Place	DIED Date	Place	MARRIED TO Date	Place
1								
2								
3								
4								
5								
6								
7								
8								
9								
10								
11								
12								

SOURCES OF INFORMATION
or documentation

Date _____

Compiler _____

Address _____

City _____ State _____ Zip _____

P.N 404899 REV 5 96

Chart provided by 20th Century Plastics. (Page 152)

Interview older family members and write down their impressions and stories as a record for future generations. As with class reunions, include a directory with names, addresses and phone numbers. Family members will appreciate the inclusion of birthdays and anniversary dates.

Many books, magazines, genealogy organizations and resources in libraries are on the Internet that can help you plan and organize a family history.

FAMILY TREE VIDEO

Another popular souvenir is to capture the reunion on video. A filmed documentary will connect family members through generations and provide a visual chronicle for posterity. A video could be prepared for an upcoming reunion or as an ongoing project adding more information and pictures as they conduct more research and additional memorabilia become available.

Your video could be a contemporary anthology including interviews of family members and adding current photos and graphics. Depending upon the time and money you have to devote to this project, it could be more elaborate and cover several generations. It could also be a "creation in process" that evolves over time and gets updated at family reunions.

Perhaps someone in your family has a video camera who can conduct interviews at the reunion and then have it professionally edited and duplicated. Trying to save money by relying on an amateur family member might not be the ideal situation. You might get what you pay for. Moreover, many opportunities could be missed with someone who is directly involved in reunion activities.

A specialist will have better equipment and assemble a more professional product by incorporating music, graphics and captions. Vintage 8 or 16-millimeter film of older home movies, slides and photographs can enhance the final product. This could be the perfect chance to commit your old photos, videos and slides to permanent history and to share the final version with relatives that couldn't make the reunion.

You could also hire professional videographers to produce a family video. Again, whoever you hire should be experienced and bonded. Don't trust personal artifacts, original photos and important records to just anyone. Preview a sample of their work to ascertain their quality and know what to expect.

If the cost makes hiring a professional prohibitive, consider creating your own video with the advice and direction of experts. A woman who was about to attend her family's 50-year reunion inspired a wonderful family video. Originally, Mary Lou Peterson's intention was to put her family's genealogy, history, stories and old photographs on video.   The project grew to include titles, background music, sound effects and narration to help tell the story of her family leaving Norway and settling in the Midwest.

Her venture led to the production of the "Gift of Heritage," an instructional video designed to help others record their family histories on video. It has hints on researching, planning and organizing materials and how to combine family tree information, photographs and slides. Basically, you learn how to tell your family's story.

Her video has interesting snippets of eight generations of her family using portraits and a drawing of the ship bringing her ancestors to the United States in the 1860s. The sound of the sea wind blowing even accents the video. Throughout the video, a narrator tells the family's story of the hardships they faced and the accomplishments they achieved. Details on how to obtain this video are in our Resource section.

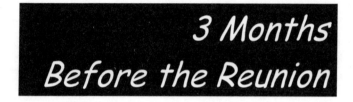

*3 Months
Before the Reunion*

11
Countdown
The Final Quarter

Continue the phone drive and editing the personal histories. Volunteer help is crucial right now, so ask committee members for help with these final tasks.

REMINDER NOTICES
Send out postcard reminder notices 4 to 6 weeks before the reunion to all "Found" alumni and friends who haven't sent in their tickets payments yet. (See sample on following page.)

NAME TAGS
The phone drive should be continuing even this close to the event. Some still have not heard about the reunion. However, you should have a substantial list of paid guests by now and if you are making your own name tags, begin making tags for those who have paid so far.

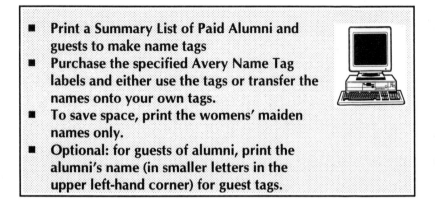

- **Print a Summary List of Paid Alumni and guests to make name tags**
- **Purchase the specified Avery Name Tag labels and either use the tags or transfer the names onto your own tags.**
- **To save space, print the womens' maiden names only.**
- **Optional: for guests of alumni, print the alumni's name (in smaller letters in the upper left-hand corner) for guest tags.**

It is very common to receive an influx of ticket payments days before the reunion, so try to prepare as many name tags as you can ahead of time. It is even a good idea to make name tags for those who suggested probable attendance as well. If they don't show up, save the tags as evidence of no-shows when you do the final tallying after the reunion.

DON'T BE LEFT OUT!
THERE ARE ONLY
5 WEEKS REMAINING
to the
Joseph's Family Reunion

When: August 12 - 16, 2000
Where: Montecito Sequoia Lodge
Cost: $420 adults, $320 children

Your reservation was accepted with your deposit. Please send in balance by 08/01/00

Info: call Jeff Jones (310) 820-5554
E-mail: info@reunionplanner.com

The Jeffersons
123 W. Sunnybrook Lane
West Village, CA 91436

Sample postcard reminder notice

PROGRAMS
A Printed Program

A printed program that describes reunion events can also be a souvenir. It can easily be created using an 8½ x 14" or 8½ x 11" sheet of heavy paper stock, (24 lb. paper weight is best), and folded in half. Put your school logo, family crest or military insignia on the cover along with the name, date and place of the reunion. On the inside, describe the reunion itinerary and activities. Some of the following suggestions are also possible:

U.S.S.
Marine

Roll call for all shipmates that
served on the
U.S.S. Marine, 1951-1954

SATURDAY
November 2, 2000
Social hour . . . . 6:30 p.m.
Dinner . . . . 8:00 p.m.
Presentations/Awards 9:00 p.m.
Dancing . . . . 9:30 - midnight

SUNDAY
November 3, 2000
Report for Brunch
U.S.S. Marine
10:00 a.m. - 2:00 p.m.

- ► comments sent in expressing appreciation to reunion committee members and other volunteers,

- ► names of the reunion committee members,

- ► a poem written by a member of your group,

- ► welcome special guests,

- ► anecdotes sent in from members of your group

- ► lists of headline news events, political leaders, songs, movies, prices of goods, etc. of the years you're remembering

▸ acknowledgments to donors of door prizes and awards,

▸ results of any reunion questionnaire or survey,

▸ copies of the school hymn, motto or song,

▸ reunion mementos offered for sale,

▸ picture of the school, family homestead or military insignia.

For more suggested contents, see Chapter 6 under Memory Albums.

A Spoken Program

Any kind of program that includes comments or announcements occur just as people are finishing a meal usually during dessert and before dancing begins. It may be the one time during the evening everyone's attention is focused on one activity. Some reunion committees prefer not to take any time away from guest's reminiscing and don't have any program. However, some sort of program is usually planned at most reunions, if only to make short announcements. For example, it is the opportune time to relate additional reunion activities, give away door prizes and awards, make presentations or introductions of special guests and first timers show a video or slides, acknowledge the committee and pronounce raffle winners.

Keep the program short, punchy and focused. The key word here is **short**. Speeches are **not** recommended, unless they are brief remarks from invited teachers or guests. Long orations are not necessary or desired at reunions who would rather be reminiscing. Keep a slide show, video or other visual portion of your program, at a minimum too.

Your DJ or band leader can act as master of ceremonies if necessary. Discuss this responsibility with the entertainer before the reunion. If you have a jukebox or prefer to handle the program on your own, make sure a podium and microphone are available. Hotels and restaurants usually provide these items at no additional charge.

Create a rough draft of your program notes. Once the final draft is completed and if others will be speaking, give them a copy with their section highlighted.

Announcements

These could include details on the picnic or other related events. Remind guests to get their pictures taken, purchase raffle tickets, help with the next reunion, send in address changes or read special letters and telegrams.

Acknowledgments, Introductions and Presentations

Thank everyone individually who contributed to the planning of the reunion, donated door prizes or went beyond the call of duty. Introduce any special guests and present plaques or commemorations. Ask someone to take still pictures of special presentations for inclusion in your photo book or memory album.

Awards

Past a certain age group, some award categories may cease to be interesting. However, some awards may still be appropriate for your group. Ask committee members what they think.

If you want to give away awards for noteworthy achievements, begin a preliminary list. Reread the personal histories and questionnaires and choose tentative award winners. As more responses arrive, winners of these awards may need to be revised.

> **Program Notes:**
> - Welcome everyone!
> - $850 raised for social action project
> - Alumni came from 12 different states to be here tonight
> - Introduce and thank committee members
> - Present gifts to attending teachers
> - Read telegrams
> - Introduce speaker
> - Choose raffle tickets winners
> - Announce door prize winners
> - Remind everyone to wear name tags at all events

▸ Married the longest

- Most recently married

- Traveled the furthest to the reunion

- Lives closest to the school, homestead or military base

- Most children, grandchildren

- Nearest to being a parent

- Nearest to being a grandparent

- First people to buy a reunion ticket

- People who attended the most reunions

- Most unique occupation

- The hardest working reunion planner (maybe the committee will surprise you on this one)

- Changed the least (This prize can be chosen the evening of the event with nominations during the program.)

You may come up with more categories, but please, keep them tactful. Don't award a prize for "the least hair," "changed the most" or "married the most." The winner would probably not appreciate such recognition.

Door Prizes
Select ticket stubs for door prize winners. At Valerie Anderson's 10-year high school reunion in Soldotna, Alaska she told us that rather than deal with raffle tickets, she wrote everyone's name who had paid on slips of paper and randomly drew them. To claim their prize, the winners had to get up in front of the group during the program and give a two-minute narration of their life in the previous ten years.

DONATIONS
If anyone responded to your questionnaire volunteering to provide prizes for goods or services, call them and graciously

acknowledge their generous donation. If applicable, verify that they will bring the item to the reunion or make arrangements for items to be picked up. If door prizes are as services, describe them on nicely designed coupons.

Gift Certificate

The Bearer of this Certificate is entitled to:

_____

Expires: _____ *Estimated Value* _____

Complements of: _____

Address: _____

Contact: _____ *Telephone:* _____

A sample certificate for donated services.

Purchase any needed door prizes that require monograms or inscriptions. Items don't have to be expensive; attendees will appreciate any creative memento. If you aren't making tickets, purchase the double stubbed "movie tickets" available in most party stores with matching numbers that can be used for selecting door prize winners or as raffle tickets.

You Get Only One First Impression, Make it Inviting.

Planning and setting up decorations and displays take forethought, people power and time management skills. Depending on how soon the banquet room is accessible, putting up elaborate decorations on the day of the reunion may be impossible. Consider the time available and plan accordingly.

If anyone on the committee is artistic, solicit their help in making welcome and informational signs for the registration area. Time permitting, include a picture or drawing of the school mascot, family crest or military logo. Samples signs are:

▸ *Welcome Los Angeles High School Romans Class of 1950*

▸ *Prepaid Tickets*

- *Will Call Tickets*

- *Photo Line Starts Here or Take Photos Here*

- *Reunion Items for Sale*

- *Raffle Tickets for Commemorative Bottle of Wine. $1.00 each*

- *Drink Tickets Sold Here*

- *First Timers Register Here*

- *After checking in, please get your picture taken for the Memory Book*

Any displays, banner or wall hangings must be removed at the end of the evening. Table centerpieces can be offered to the guests, but someone from the committee should be responsible for collecting all other decorations and memorabilia. **A very reliable person needs to be in charge of the cash box.** If you are at a hotel, restaurant or museum, ask the manager to lock the cash box in a safe deposit box when the registration tables close.

12
Final Arrangements
The Final Weeks

A s you head down the stretch toward the finish line, before getting too focused on the winning post, be aware of some sideline activities, for our purposes, loose ends. Besides updating the guest list and completing the name tags, handouts and other displays, start assembling the registration packets. Begin putting together the packets as soon as possible because you'll likely be finishing them right up to the last minute.

THE GUEST LIST

The attendance list should be sizeable by now. Prepare a preliminary list of paid guests with names of all attendees, the number in each group and the amounts paid. This list will be very helpful at the registration tables. If you don't have a computer program, create this initial list with a pencil (there will be changes). Since ticket payments will trickle in at the last minute, the final attendee list can be printed the day before the reunion.

■ **Print a summary list of paid alumni without guest names. This list includes alumni's name, phone numbers and the paid attendance total for each alumnus.**

LOOSE ENDS

Check on the completion of the following assignments.

❑ handmade signs,

❑ decorations and table centerpieces,

❑ reminding donors who are bringing door prizes. If contributions are in the form of services, describe them on nicely printed coupons (page 167). Have an extra bottle of wine in case someone forgets to bring their donation.

❑ verification of persons working the registration table, with notes listing their responsibilities,

❑ floral arrangements.

Verify the attendance and arrival time of all vendors.

❑ the entertainer (make sure the DJ or band leader has your song list and will play **your** designated selections

❑ videographer,

❑ photographer,

❑ T-shirts and others.

Finally, check that invited guests have the reunion time and location information and arrange for their hotel rooms, if applicable. If your budget allows, offer to pay for their room if they are arriving from out of town.

. . . TWO MORE WEEKS

This should be the deadline for making changes in anything going to a printer or other document. Corrections in your current selection of award winners must wait for the next reunion.

Memory Album, Handouts and Displays

Deliver the camera-ready draft of the memory album, family history chronicle, program, T-shirt or other handout to your printer. Make sure you have sufficient time to receive the final product before the reunion. Waiting until this late date enables you to include many last minute submissions. **Always allow extra time for the delivery of the final product because unforeseen delays always occur. Allow several hours for final proofreading. Check the spelling of names and that the information is credited with the right person.**

The banner, posters and any other prizes should be in hand by now. If you have a slide show or video presentation, go through a rehearsal to verify that the slides are in proper order and show time is kept to the designated time frame. (Remember: The entire program should not last more than twenty minutes.)

MAIL TICKETS

Do not wait later than two weeks before the reunion to mail out tickets, first class of course. The U.S. Mail system can be unpredictable, so don't take the risk of tickets being lost in the mail this close to the reunion. If you are using bulk rate mail, and we suggest that you don't, allow at least a month for delivery. This mode of mail service has been known to take even longer to reach their destinations.

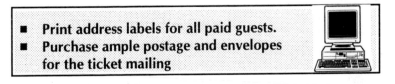

- **Print address labels for all paid guests.**
- **Purchase ample postage and envelopes for the ticket mailing**

When sending out tickets, you might include an outline of the reunion itinerary. Send the itinerary to those who responded that they will be attending other reunion activities.

REGISTRATION

If you hired professional planners, they will handle the entire registration process and you can skip this section.

Registration Packets

After updating the guest list with any last minute ticket purchases, prepare an updated attendance list. Depending upon the quantity and dimensions of the registrations packet contents, get envelopes that are proportionate. Three or four people can fill the packets in a few hours.

Put the guest names and the number of paid tickets on the outside of each envelope. If any guests owe a balance or for those who said they would pay at the door, highlight the phrase **"Balance Due $50.00"** in red on the envelope. (See the sample below.) These envelopes will be at the Will Call table. This conspicuous reminder will help the person collecting payments of the amount due so they don't have to take time calculating.

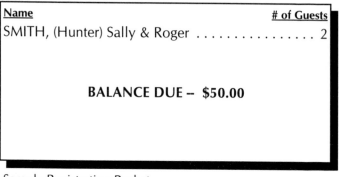

Sample Registration Packet

Name Tags

Include name tags for the spouses and guests of the main person for class and military reunions. For family reunions as an alternative to pre-made name tags, guests can create their own tags as a craft activity.

Tip: Prepare extra registration packets for those who said they might attend (hold these at the Will Call table). It won't take that much extra effort to prepare and the packets will be ready when and if they show up.

Refunds or Prepaid Purchase Items

Insert any refunds that may be due. Check-in volunteers can hand out any reunion souvenirs that were part of the ticket price: class directory, a memory album, video, CD, etc., along with the packets.

If tickets were mailed out and some people paid too late to have their tickets sent to them, put these prepaid tickets in the registration envelopes.

REGISTRATION TABLES

A smooth-operating registration process is essential. No one wants to spend a lot of time checking in. Once people start to see familiar faces, they'll want to start gabbing. So, organize the check-in process to be quick and painless. Everyone will appreciate it. Have the following items available:

▸ Alphabetized Registration Packets

▸ An alphabetical list of all prepaid attendees with number of guests and amounts paid

▸ List of Will Call guests

▸ A reunion program, memory albums, family history books and/or other hand outs

▸ To reduce waiting in line even further, prepare large block letters in two or three alphabetical sections. For example, if 200 or more people are attending and depending upon the available space and number registration volunteers, try forming three lines such as: **A - H, I - R** and **S - Z.**

Tip: See if the facility has stands to display these signs behind each letter grouping.

▸ Blank name tags and someone with good writing skills to make them on the spot

▸ Pens, pencils, blank envelopes, tape, paper clips, scissors, stapler and staples

▸ A cash box with change including some ones, fives and ten dollar bills for the Will Call table and for raffle ticket purchases

▸ Door prize tickets

▸ A wastepaper basket

▸ Container for raffle tickets and/or door prize ticket stubs

Tip: One committee bought three rolls of ticket stubs in different colors. They used blue for the dinner tickets, red for raffle tickets and orange for door prizes. The dinner tickets were single and the red and orange ticket rolls had two stubs each. Everyone got a door prize ticket in their packets. Upon entering, the door prize ticket stubs were collected. They also sold raffle tickets. Then they put the stubs for each drawing into two different shoe boxes.

Check-in Responsibilities

To promote an orderly reception process with the least amount of waiting time, designate assignments and write down the schedule for each worker. Explain it again as they are sitting with the information in front of them. Spouses of committee workers can help if there aren't enough people at the check-in table. (Even if enough volunteers promised to help, someone may not show up or arrive too late.)

A one-hour shift is the maximum time anyone should work at the check in tables. Provide for a second shift or relief assistance if the check-in process lasts more than an hour. The tables needn't be manned for the entire evening. However, it is not fair for people to show up after dinner and not expect to pay anything. **Those who arrive after dinner should be charged part of the ticket price since there are many other costs associated with the reunion besides the meal cost.** Come up with an amount to charge those who show up at the last minute or after dinner.

If you are planning your own event, getting people to man the check-in tables when they are anxious to join in the festivities will be difficult. Perhaps the facility has their own guards that can monitor the area, but they won't be noticing late arrivals that look like they belong there.

WILL CALL

Will Call transactions should be handled separately from the prepaid registrants. This will greatly reduce confusion and waiting time at the check-in tables. Cash settlements take longer. This separate system enables the person handling cash transactions to concentrate on just that. With two persons helping, this area can also manage cash sales for raffle tickets.

If unreserved guests show up at the door, the registration workers should place the payments inside an envelope and designate the name of the purchaser on the envelope. **Identifying those guests who pay for their tickets with cash is especially important.** Accounting for unidentified cash ticket payments after the reunion can be very frustrating.

Staffing

Two people should be in charge of the Will Call table, one to handle monetary transactions and another to make any additional name tags and tear off any door prize ticket stubs. Memory albums or other handouts should also be available at this table. **The cash box should always be under supervision or in a safe place.**

Final Meeting Agenda

1. Call respondents who haven't paid
2. Stuff registration envelopes
3. Day assignments:
- set up
  2:00 - 4:00,   Stan, John
  4:00 - 6:00,   Bev, Bob
- registration table
  6:30 - 7:30,   Lynn, Tim
  7:30 - 8:00,   Cindy, Mike
- will call
  6:30 - 7:30,   Stan, Rob
  7:30 - 8:00,   Jamie
- clean up: Susan, Bob, Stan

Prepaid Registration

Besides cheerfully greeting people, volunteer responsibilities include the following:

▸ Handing out registration packets

▸ Handing out prepaid items as memory albums, program or other prepared booklet. (Or, place programs at each place setting.)

▸ Direct guests toward the photographer to have their pictures taken. (The photographer should make sure pictures are taken without name tags.)

▸ If there are door prize tickets, separate the tickets and put stubs in a container or bowl.

FINAL ARRANGEMENTS WITH THE FACILITY OR CATERER
Meal Count

The catering manager will require a meal count guarantee and may even want full payment a week before the event. Use the paid list and estimate a few more for those who promised to pay at the door. Most restaurant facilities can accommodate up to a 7 percent overage of your guarantee (check with the facility) in accounting for unexpected guests.

Don't overestimate the number of unexpected arrivals because the inevitable no-shows will balance the few unannounced guests. Refunds are not usually requested, or for that matter, offered at reunions. The time, effort and additional cost factors that reunion committees incur more than compensate for paid no-shows. Nevertheless, if there is an emergency or enough notice is received, try to accommodate people with some amount.

Work out a diagram of how the tables should be set up including the registration tables so there will be no confusion or lengthy discussions during the reunion. You will be very grateful

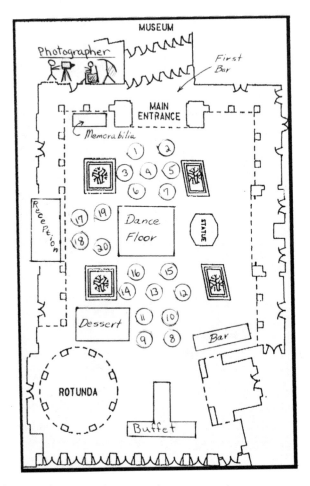

Sample room layout with seating for 200 people.

for any details that can be worked out in advance that will avert potential last minute problems or surprises. This diagram will also serve as a great help for the management and meal caterer. If you hired an off-site caterer, a prepared layout will be very helpful at least two weeks in advance and faxed to the caterer.

Equipment

Confirm availability of the following items with the reunion facility. Hopefully, when negotiating your contract, you were able to get much of the following equipment included in the overall fee. Any additional costs should already be accounted for in your budget. However, it's wise to verify with the facility that any other items will be available.

▸   Registration tables

▸   Stands for holding letters or signs

▸   Easels and/or bulletin boards for posters, pictures and other displays

▸   Podium and microphone

▸   Dance floor

▸   Plenty of water pitchers (so your guests don't always have to pay for drinks to quench their thirst).

▸   A place to hang your banner

▸   Screen for slide show

▸   A/V equipment

▸   Containers for door prize and raffle ticket stubs

CONTINGENCY PLAN

An emergency plan should be set up for someone to take over decision making and overall management of the reunion in case a key person is unable to attend the reunion. At least one other person should be aware of the evening's responsibilities and prepared to take over.

IF IT LOOKS LIKE YOUR RUNNING SHORT

Remember, don't ask for donations to help defray reunion expenses at the reunion. Hopefully, you budgeted well so that expenses have not exceeded revenues and enough people have signed up to cover all costs. However, in the event you are running short, refer to some suggestions described in Chapter 4, under Revenues for help in raising last minute cash.

If a shortage occurs at a family reunion, a last minute appeal in the mail may bring in the necessary cash. Illustrate the shortage as a per person amount. You may get a larger donation from some family members to make up for those who really can't afford to contribute anymore.

The Reunion Event

13

It's Reunion Time

R-Day is Here!

The moment you have been waiting for has finally arrived! This chapter provides a scenario and an approximate time frame of reunion events.

Make sure committee members know their expected arrival time and when to be available for the committee picture. Give yourselves extra time to set up the banquet room. If you won't be returning home or to a hotel room, bring your reunion attire.

REUNION DAY CHECK LIST

Copy the list on the following page and check off the items as they are taken care of. We highlighted the really important items. Fill the blanks with items of your own.

- **Under Checklists, print Event-Day Check List.**

	Items to Bring		Things to Do
✔	Registration packets		Set up table centerpieces
✔	Memory albums, programs		Set up decorations, posters
✔	Cash Box with change		Arrange registration packets
✔	List of paid guests		Hang banners, etc.
	Registration/direction signs		Reserve a table for yourself and committee members
	Memorabilia, photo collage, other displays		Meet with and go over duties with registration desk workers
	Extra Tickets		Take committee pictures before reunion gets underway
	Blank Name Tags		Confirm meal arrangements and serving time frame with catering manager
	Stapler, Scotch Tape	✔	Reaffirm your song list with DJ
	Pens and Pencils		Meet with vendors
	Banner		Get dressed
	Posters, other decor		Relax and have fun
	Table Centerpieces		
	Door Prizes		
	Awards or Certificates		
	Receipt book		
	Reunion Checkbook		
✔	Personal Program Notes		
	Camera for candid pictures		
✔	Reunion Clothes		

✔   These are absolutely essential

Optional or As Necessary
❐ Easels/Bulletin Boards. (If the facility doesn't provide them)
❐ Slide Show Equipment
❐ Video Tape Equipment

Based on responses from class, family and military reunion organizers, a scenario on how a typical reunion weekend might unfold is outlined below.

FRIDAY NIGHT
Opening reception in hospitality suite . . . . 7:00 p.m.

Introductory activities . . . . 8:00 p.m.

Ice breakers . . . . 9:00 p.m.

SATURDAY
Breakfast . . . . 8:00 a.m.

Sports tournaments . . . . 10:00 to noon

Lunch (on own) . . . . Noon

Off-site tours . . . . 1:00 - 5:00 p.m.

At the Reunion Facility
▶ Set up table centerpieces, posters, decorations and other displays

▶ Organize check-in tables with alphabetized registration packets

▶ Hang banners

▶ Get dressed

Coordinate the Evening's Agenda
▶ Greet and discuss the evening's agenda with catering manager, photographer and entertainer.

▶ Discuss with the entertainer if they will act as Master of Ceremonies or make any introductions. Remind the entertainer to consider the focus of the event and keep the music level *low*. (After all, this is *your* reunion. Insist on this.)

- Find out how late the photographer will be available to take guest pictures and still have time to take candid shots.

- Go over responsibilities and time commitments with registration desk workers.

Evening Banquet

- Take committee picture and committee family portraits before guests arrive.

        Social hour . . . . *6:30 - 8:00 p.m.*

- Someone from the reunion committee should supervise the registration process and make sure the cash box is in a safe place at all times.

        Dinner . . . . *8:00 - 9:30 p.m.*

        Program . . . . *9:10 - 9:30 p.m.*

Sample Program Agenda. (Refer to your notes)

- Welcome everyone

- Thank committee members

- Introduce special guests

- ▸ Read important letters or telegrams
- ▸ Show video or slides
- ▸ Make announcements
- ▸ Present awards
- ▸ Select door prize winners
- ▸ Discuss itinerary for other reunion events
- ▸ Remind attendees to wear name badges at all reunion events
- ▸ Request volunteers for the next reunion
- ▸ Thank everyone for coming

  Dancing and Reminiscing . . . . *9:30 p.m. – ?*

Before Leaving the Event

- ▸ Retrieve cash box, banner, posters, registration supplies and memorabilia
- ▸ Pay facility or caterer for balance due.

SUNDAY

Brunch . . . . *10:00 a.m. to 1:00 p.m.*

▸ Speakers
▸ Auction (if not held Saturday)
▸ Collect quilt squares, recipes, photos for next reunion

Items for Additional Events

Having more than one reunion event presents an opportunity for people to bring their families and continue reminiscing. It also allows many of whom were unable to attend the dinner/dance a chance to participate in another reunion activity.

If the cost of a Sunday meal was not included in the original ticket price, and a picnic is planned, remind people to bring their own lunches and sports equipment. Items for the committee to bring:

▸ Banner
▸ Bar-b-que and accompaniments (if necessary)
▸ Lunch or snacks
▸ Memory books and other souvenirs for new arrivals
▸ Reunion sale items and receipt book
▸ Camera (for more candid shots)

14

It's Not Over Yet

Congratulations, you successfully put on a milestone event! Except for a few loose ends, you can officially consider this masterful job, done.

CLOSING COSTS AND RESPONSIBILITIES

The only financial liability remaining should be the final payment to the photographer for the preparation and mailing of the photo albums. Payment will probably be required at the time you send in the paste up of the photo album (described below).

PHOTO BOOK

This project should be completed as soon as possible. Everyone will appreciate receiving the photo book with names and addresses while the reunion afterglow is still alive. In this way, people may quickly follow through on contacts made at the reunion.

The photographer should send the picture proofs within a few weeks after the reunion. The proofs should come with instructions on what is necessary to process the booklet. Upon receiving the proofs, verify that they spelled each person's name correctly and matched the right photograph. Listed below are some ideas for individual pages:

Introductory Page

- ▸ Brief statement thanking everyone who attended the reunion and why it was so successful.

- ▸ Reunion facts: Name, date and place of reunion

- ▸ Picture of school, class insignia, family crest or military logo

- ▸ List of award winners such as *"Who Traveled the Farthest to the Reunion?"*

- ▸ Names of committee members

- ▸ A statement about the next reunion

- ▸ A memorial page

- ▸ Contact address and phone number for future reunion information

- ▸ Roster or directory of names and addresses.

> ■ **Print the entire roster with your group's names and addresses in a small font so as not to use up several pages of the photo book.**

If you prepared a memory album, you may have already used some photo book suggestions above. However, if you are combining a photo book with a memory album, refer to the design ideas in Chapter 6.

Collage Pages

Combine any pictures taken at the various reunion events and cut and paste them so several fit on one page. Depending on the number of pictures and how much space there is to fill, create the appropriate number of pages.

THANK YOU NOTES

Thank you notes should be sent to special guests, the facility event coordinator, the reunion coordinator of the school, committee members who volunteered their time, those who donated services or prizes and others deserving appreciation.

REMAINING MEMORY ALBUMS AND PHOTO BOOKS

Send memory albums and/or photo books to all those who bought them separately. Send books to those who paid to attend the reunion, but didn't show up.

A follow up letter shortly after the reunion can accomplish a few goals. (See the example on page 190.) It provides closure on the event, reminds alumni and family members to keep the committee informed of any address changes and gives them one last chance to purchase reunion items. If the letter is sent before the photo book goes out, business card ads can still be solicited. This final mailer could bring in some extra cash to cover any shortfalls or build a nest egg for the next reunion.

WRAP-UP
Bank Account

Immediately upon the close of reunion, prepare a budget review. If possible, do this the day after the reunion. Add up any receipts from the reunion event and formulate a final tally of revenues and expenses including costs yet to be paid such as the photo book.

The reunion bank account can be closed after all bills have been paid and checks have cleared. If you budgeted carefully, a balance should be remaining. Open up a savings account and keep any surplus for the next reunion. You could also divide any remaining funds among key committee members who put in an extraordinary amount of time and effort on the reunion. Another welcomed and thoughtful gesture would be to donate part of any balance to your school in honor of your class reunion. This small gesture gives back something in return for what the school gave you. It could also act as an incentive for current students.

Thank You University High Stallions
Class of 1978
For a Wonderful Reunion

Dear Alumni:

By all accounts, everyone who attended the reunion two weeks ago had a fantastic time. It was much work, but well worth the effort judging by the feedback we've received.

Reunion Video: For those of you who did not get an opportunity to purchase a video at the reunion, or did not attend and would like to see what you missed, you can purchase it for only $23.50 including postage. A professional videographer who captured the event is editing the tape now. It will be ready in approximately six weeks.

Photo Book. The memory album/photo book is also in preparation and should be completed and mailed out in approximately 8 weeks. You still have time to advertise your business card. The cost is $15.00 per card. If you would like to purchase the photo book that has pictures of everyone who attended, candid shots of the reunion and an alumni directory including E-mail addresses, the cost is also $15.00.

Address Changes. Much of our time planning reunions is spent finding people. If there are any address changes or you know the whereabouts of other fellow alum or run into anyone sometime before the next reunion, please call, write or E-mail any committee member as soon as possible so we can add them to our mailing list.

Deadline for ad in photo book is 10/25, other purchases 12/15.

Make check out to University High 25 Year Reunion and mail to:

Jeff Smith, 12345 East Lane, Lakewood, CO 80228. (303) 555-1212

Name_____Hm Phone ( )_____

Address_____Bus Phone ( )_____

_____E-mail_____

$_____Include my enclosed business card in Photo Book @ $15 each

$_____I would like a Reunion Video @ $23.50 each.

$_____I would like a Photo Book @ $15.00 each

$_____TOTAL ENCLOSED

Storage of Supplies

Put all remaining memory albums, photo books, name tags, memorabilia and other reunion files and supplies in a storage box. They will be very helpful for the next reunion, no matter who plans it.

- ■ Update and put computer program and files in safe place for the next reunion.
- ■ Contact publisher for updates.

REFLECT AND REVISE

In the next few weeks, while everything is still fresh in your mind, write down everyone's thoughts on the reunion, what went well and what needed improvement. This will be helpful for the next reunion game plan.

Plan a post reunion committee gathering. Have a potluck dinner at a committee member's home and show the reunion video. Everyone will be busy reminiscing about the reunion, so this will also be a good time to collect more ideas.

- ▶ Should the reunion start earlier, last longer?

- ▶ Was the menu interesting and should we change it to a buffet or sit-down?

- ▶ Did the registration process run smoothly?

- ▶ Were there any mishaps?

- ▶ Could any expenditures be eliminated or added?

THE POST REUNION BLUES

If you suffer from *post reunion let down*, consider doing a follow up project. If there are any funds left over, save some for postage on a periodic newsletter or ask for subscription donations to cover postage costs. This continued contact will promote continued interest and help to keep the mailing list current. Tulsa Central High School in Tulsa, Oklahoma puts out a quarterly newsletter to all graduates of classes as far back as 1934. They offer newsy stories about the high school, raise funds for a foundation for school programs and keep alumni posted on upcoming reunions and events. They include memorials and maintain address records.

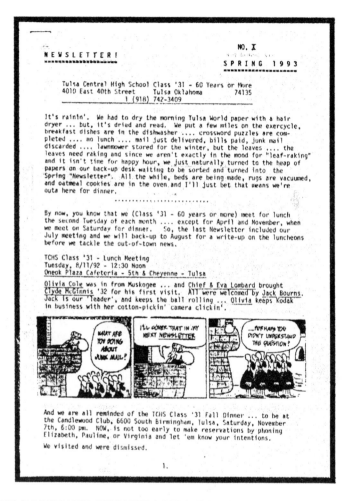

KEEP IN TOUCH BETWEEN REUNIONS

By maintaining contact via a newsletter or other correspondence, you maintain the lists you worked so hard to create. If there is enough money to cover printing and postage costs, consider sending a follow-up letter to the entire group. You offer those who missed the events or who didn't have a chance during the reunion to purchase any memorabilia items that were sold or any final photo book of the reunion itself.

15

Stay Up to Date with Reunion Planning

Keep the Reunion Ambiance Alive

Now that the reunion is past, don't let the excitement and enthusiasm dissipate. Stay up to date with reunion planning by checking the Internet, the library and book stores for updates and new ideas. Besides the reunion related Websites mentioned throughout this book, more associations and related support services will open up.

Alumni, family and friends will be looking forward to the next reunion. If you plan on passing the torch to someone else next time, lend them your support and information. If you will be the one initiating the next reunion, keep abreast of the latest time saving techniques and developments.

Many may think the next reunion can't possibly surpass the previous one. Don't believe it. With your experience and know how, the next reunion will be even better. Visit our Website for new ideas, links to more reunion-related sites and for future reunion announcements: ***http://www.reunionplanner.com.*** At the same time, share your expertise with other reunion organizers. It is in everyone's best interest. May your lives be blessed with many happy reunions.

Before you close the book on your reunion, please take a moment and complete the survey on the next page. We really appreciate your feedback and want to hear about your reunion experiences.

Survey

Please take a moment to complete this survey. *Even if only some questions are answered, we would appreciate your responses.* Tell us about some of your reunion experiences. Just copy this form, complete it and either mail or fax your responses to the publisher. Simpler yet, respond to the survey on our Website at ***www.reunionplanner.com/survey.*** All avenues to contact us appear at the end of this survey.

Please include any interesting stories or anecdotes under Additional Comments.

Type or reason for reunion_____
                (30th high school, 50th wedding anniversary, annual military, etc.)

Place held _____
                (Hotel, restaurant, etc.)

Date of reunion _____

Frequency and duration of reunion:_____

Number of attendees _____

What methods were used to locate people?_____

_____

How were people notified about the reunion?_____

_____

Were some guests resistant to attending the reunion? Why? _____

_____

_____

What was the ticket price? _____

What other events were planned if the reunion occurred for more than a day?

_____

_____

What displays and/or decorations were there?_____

_____

Were there additional fundraising activities? If so, what?_____

_____

What activities or games were planned? _____

_____

What type of entertainment was provided? _____

Were there any special guests or former teachers in attendance?

_____

What, if any, awards or door prizes were offered? _____

_____

Were souvenirs included as part of the ticket price? For example, programs, photo books, T-shirts, coffee mugs, caps?

_____

_____

Were there any items available to purchase?_____

_____

What did you like the most about the reunion?_____

_____

What did you like the least?_____

_____

Is there anything you would improve upon?_____

_____

Is there anything you'd like to see covered in future editions?

_____

Name _____

School or Organization_____

If we use any of your comments in the next edition, would you like to be credited? If so, please sign here.

☐_____
    Yes, you have permission to use my name with any of my comments
    that are used in the next edition of *The Reunion Planner.*

☐   Please send updates on the latest Reunion Planner products or
    information to:

Name/E-mail/Website_____

Address_____

City _____State _____Zip_____

ADDITIONAL COMMENTS

_____

_____

_____

_____

_____

_____

_____

_____

_____

_____.

Thank you for your comments. Please send or fax your comments to us at the address below or contact us through our Website: **www.reunionplanner.com**

Goodman Lauren Publishing
11661 San Vicente Boulevard
Los Angeles, California 90049
(800) 899-6978
(310) 820-8341 *fax*

Resources

Listed below are references to reunion locations, vendors and information. Many of these resources are referred to throughout the book. The related page numbers are indicated when applicable.

Badges

Badge A Mint. Manufacturer of button-making equipment. Call for brochure 800-223-4103

Tempbadge Plus. Paper badges without holders, clips or pins. 800-628-0022

Cookbooks

Cookbook Publishers. Call for information kit: 800-227-7282. pg. 140

Family Tree Software

Broderbund. For general questions or ordering software: 800-315-0672 or, www.familytreemaker.com. pg. 60, 152

Family History Products

Everton Publishers. Call for free catalogue: 800-443-6325. pgs. 59, 151

Family Chronicle. Magazine for families researching their roots. 416-696-5488, famchron@moorshead.com. pgs. 152-3

Heritage Quest. Call for free catalogue. 800-760-2455. pgs. 151-2

Locations

Battlefield Tours: 800-635-5018. pg. 147

Battleship Massachusetts: 800-533-3194. pg. 147

Forever Resorts. Houseboat Vacation Rentals: 800-255-5561. pg. 41

Fort Robinson: Frontier reunions: 308-665-2900. pg. 41

Fort Worden: Frontier reunions: 360-385-4730. pg. 41

Houseboat Association of America. List of rental agencies. 803-744-6581. Bobperkins@aol.com. pg. 40

Montecito Sequoia: National Forest & Lodge. Office: 800-227-9900 or Lodge: 800-843-8677. www.montecitosequoia.com. pg. 38

Native American Reservation Bureaus. Santa Fe, New Mexico Convention and Visitors Bureau, 800-777-2849

Steamboatin' Historic Tours of America, 714-846-6446. pg. 39

Valor Tours. Pacific and European cruises: 415-332-7850. pg. 147

YMCA of the Rockies. For group planning guide, 800-777-YMCA

Memorabilia

Hollywood Movie Posters. Movie posters shipped anywhere. Open 11a.m. - 5:00 p.m. Monday - Saturday. 323-463-1792. pg.126

National Pen Corporation. Custom pens and other products. Call for free brochure. 800-854-1000.

Military Service Personnel
Women in Military Service Memorial, Dept. 560
Washington DC 20042-0560, 800-4-SALUTE. *This foundation is seeking names, addresses, photos and experiences of women who have served in the armed services. The Memorial will appear at the gateway to Arlington National Cemetery. Descendants and friends of deceased servicewomen are asked to register them.*

Quilting Starter Kits
Spirited Hands. Call for info: 253-922-4523

Reunion Planners
Black Family Reunions. Sponsored by the National Council of Negro Women, 202-463-6680. pg. 135
National Association of Reunion Managers. 800-654-2776. www.reunions.com. info@reunions.com. pgs. 11, 61

Reunion Articles, Information and Services
Complete Reunion Planner, The. Software and book to help plan class family & military reunions. 800-899-6978. www.reunionplanner.com
Family History Centers. 800-346-6044. pgs. 150-2
Family Reunion Handbook. Brown & Ninkovich. Family reunion guide and resources, *Military Reunion Handbook.* Masciangelo & Ninkovich. Good reference for military reunion planning. Reunion Research: 3145 Geary Blvd. #14 San Francisco, CA 94118. www.reuniontips.com. pg. 3
National Reunion Registry and Press Services. Sends press announcements: 210-438-4177. pg. 148
Reunions Magazine. Quarterly magazine with stories on family, class & military reunions. 414-263-4567. www.reunionmag.com. pgs. 3, 60, 148, 205

Videography Products and Information
Mary Lou Productions: P.O. Box 17233 Minneapolis, MN 55417. Make your own family video with the Gift of Heritage demonstration video. 800-774-8511. www.giftofheritage.com. pgs. 158, 205
Raines Video Productions: 800-654-8277. Specializes in producing high school reunions. pg. 92
Wonder Stories. Documents oral family histories on video. Will travel, call for prices: 310-455-2142.

Wine with Custom Labels
Windsor Vineyards: 800-Buy-Wine or 800-289-9463. pgs. 123-4

Index

Save time and get results fast!

The Reunion Planner is a detailed, step-by-step guide to reunion planning. A time-line organizes suggestions and directions, taking planners through a 12-month action plan, from first contacts to the event itself. Easy-to-use checklists, sample questions for vendors and a sample budget are all included.

An easy-to-use software program is also available, making it easy to handle data, budgets, label printing and more.

Linda Johnson Hoffman is an event planner based in Los Angeles. In addition to organizing fund raisers and political campaign dinners, she has helped plan many class reunions. Neal Barnett is a systems analyst in the Bay Area, California. He makes computers work with equal ease for information managers and alumni planners.

YES!

I'd like to order *The Complete Reunion Planner* software program.

Copy and send or fax this page.
Requirements: PC computer, Windows 95/98/NT™ installed.
10 MB HD space, 8 MB RAM. Designed to support all printers.

❏ Software only   _____ x $24.95 = $ _____
❏ Software and book package   _____ x $29.95 = $ _____
❏ Book only   _____ x $14.95 = $ _____

                           Shipping via UPS   5.00
                           Subtotal $ _____
California residents add sales tax @ 8.25%   _____
                           Grand Total $ _____

Name: _____
Address: _____
City: _____ State _____ Zip: _____
Phone: _____ E-mail: _____

Make checks payable to:
Goodman Lauren Publishing
11661 San Vicente Blvd., Los Angeles, California 90049
or, Call toll free (800) 899-6978 or fax (310) 820-8341
Order directly from our Website: www.reunionplanner.com